**More powerful tha[...]
well, anything**

D1589543

FATHER POWER

Inspiring Every Dad to be His
Child's Superhero

TODD WILSON

ISBN-10: 1-933858-17-6

ISBN-13: 978-1-933858-17-3

Scripture quotations are taken from the HOLY BIBLE, NEW INTERNA-TIONAL VERSION. Copyright © 1973, 1978, 1984 by International Bible Society. Used by permission of Zondervan.

All inquiries should be addressed to: Familyman Ministries, 611 S. Main St., Milford, IN 46542

Printed in the United States of America

To My Dad

You gave me a great example to follow and demonstrated many times that a man can choose what's best. You made sacrifices for our family and they paid off. I hope I grow up to be just like you...well, almost like you.

CONTENTS

FROM ME TO YOU

Dad,

I think fathering is the coolest, yet most demanding, thankless, overwhelming job on the planet. It is also the most important job you will ever...I mean EVER have.

I know you want to do your best, but I also know that there are many pressures pulling you in a dozen different directions. You have dreams and ambitions, goals and aspirations, and a wife who wants you to be more involved with your kids and take a greater role in leading your family.

I know all this because I'm faced with the exact same pressures.

My goal in writing this book is to impress upon you the incredible power that you hold in your hand. It's called Father Power, and it is the power that affects millions. As soon

After 8 trips to the car, 7 pillows, 13 stuffed animals, 9 toothbrushes, 8 suitcases, and 4 special blankees, Bob looked longingly at the businesssman who stepped onto the elevator.

as your first child enters the world, you automatically possess this power.

As I write this book, a sense of urgency pushes me along.

Can you hear that? Time is passing.

Shut your eyes, take a deep breath, and listen carefully as it passes. Seconds tick by, adding up to minutes, days, weeks, months, years, and lifetimes.

Unfortunately, most of us dads have quit listening. The busyness of work, life, and the world around us has clogged our ears. But whether we notice or not, time continues to pass, often leaving regrets and "I should haves" in its path.

We get so caught up in what's important to us that we forget what's really important, and I don't want you to get to the end of your life with major regrets in the fathering department.

You know what? Things that seem so important to us at age 30 and 40 will seem so unimportant at 70, 80, and 90. That's because when you get old, everything seems to come into focus and suddenly the world becomes clearer.

That's why I like to hang out with old guys. They have a perspective on life that enables them to remind guys like me to enjoy my kids before it's too late.

I wonder how many old dads would kill to have the chance to do it all over again? Many have regrets about the time they spent away from home, on the road, or working to build a career. Perhaps they rushed through parenting longing for their kids to grow up, not realizing how much they would miss all the noise and confusion once they were gone.

Like Jacob Marley, Scrooge's dead partner in *A Christmas Carol*, it's too late for them, but maybe there is some redemption in reminding young dads about what's most important.

So, I've written this book for you, Dad, because the stakes are high, and my desire is to see you choose the best and be the dad your family deserves and you want to be. I know it's not easy. I can't write three pages in a row without getting caught up in what I think is important.

Just ten minutes ago, I had my son in tears because I got frustrated when he interrupted my work and wanted me to do something that was so...so...unimportant. When in truth, what I was doing was so unimportant compared to the time I could have invested in him. I hate that. Yet, I do it all the time.

And, I see dads all around me trading the eternally important stuff for stuff that doesn't matter squat.

Are you one of those dads?

He's a Christian dad who vocalizes his commitment to the family. He's got great looking children and a seemingly happy wife. They dress up nice on Sunday, and he even teaches an adult Sunday school class. Looking in, everyone would call him the model man. The pastor wishes he had ten men just like him. He's committed, hard working, and dependable.

These same qualities have helped him in the business world. People can count on him. He gets the job done right and doesn't quit until it's finished. But being committed does have its drawbacks. He works 60 plus hours a week, is never home for dinner, and barely makes it home in time to say goodnight to the kids.

Once he is home, there is work to be done on the computer, emails to answer, and paperwork to do. He stays up late and then rolls out of bed well before the rest of the household to slip off to the office to get more work done before things get hectic.

His wife has begged him to spend more time with them, but she has given up because it doesn't work. His kids used to cry and whine for daddy, but now they just carry on without him.

He knows that he works too much and promises that it will all change as soon as...as soon as...well, you know.

Now fast forward. The years pass by. His children grow up and move to different parts of the country. He reaches the top of the corporate ladder and retires with a stock portfolio big enough to choke Warren Buffet. He has a big home, a vacation condo, and all the comforts money can buy.

Now, he and his wife spend much of their time going out to eat. They stare at families with small kids, sad that it's all over for them.

Most of us dads fit this description. We've been fed a bunch of lies, and we've believed them lock, stock, and barrel.

Do any of these lies sound familiar?

- *A man gets his significance from his work.*
- *You have to make some sacrifices now so you can be prepared for the future.*
- *If you don't work like a dog, you're lazy.*
- *You have to work this many hours in order to do a good job for your employer.*
- *Your wife can handle it.*

- *Your children will thank you one day.*
- *You just want to give your children what you never had.*
- *You're doing it for them.*

Enough!

At the end of this book, I'm going to ask you some questions—tough questions. It's not only for your wife and children that I must ask them, but ultimately, it's for YOU. I want to help you make good rocking chair decisions...that is, the decisions that you won't regret when you're sitting in a rocking chair eating red Jell-O someday.

They are hard questions to ask, and even harder questions to answer. But I'm asking you to be honest and truthful. Then, I want you to make some choices in light of your answers.

I want to encourage you to do what millions of dads know they need to do but for a variety of reasons won't. I know you can do it. Your family is counting on you. God is counting on you, and so am I.

But before we get to the most important questions you'll ever ask yourself, let's take a look at the greatest power on the planet...you.

You 'da Dad,

Todd

MORE POWERFUL THAN A LOCOMOTIVE

Dad, you are the greatest power the world has ever known. Sure, there is the power of the INTERNET, atomic power, flower power, the power of a hug, and the power of the pen, but all of these pale in comparison to **Father Power**.

Over the past couple of decades, I've had the privilege of leading and being part of many men's groups. I've sat in circles and talked about your standard guy things like work, sports, lawn care, and carburetors.

Occasionally, the conversation transitions to spiritual issues like our relationship with God, our wife, and our kids. I've noticed that the two most passionate topics discussed are fathers and children.

Guys can talk about struggles in their marriage without batting an eye. They can feel miles away from God and still joke. Their car can be on its last leg...OK they cry on that one, but on most other topics every eye is dry.

But, ask a dad about his father, and the atmosphere in the room changes. Suddenly, men get all wishy washy and start to fidget in their seats. Some share good memories, others talk about wounds that have never healed.

I've seen grown men describe an event involving their dad that happened thirty years ago with clarity, deep emotion, and passion. Their lips quiver and their eyes glisten. Listening to them talk, you would think it had taken place a week ago, not three decades ago.

What's the reason behind such startling emotion?

Father Power.

On the other side of the pendulum, the topic of children touches just as many raw nerves. On many occasions, I've talked to dads about their children and again the tears flow quickly in men who normally show little emotion.

Why is that?

Father Power.

Father power is the power of the relationship between a father and his children for good or bad. Sociologists can try to minimize the perceived impact of father power, but it doesn't change the truth.

Our society is reeling from the gaping hole left by absentee fathers. Kids join gangs to gain the acceptance they lack from their father. Girls give away their purity and get pregnant seeking the love of a man when their dad hasn't met that need. Men pursue greatness and power trying to prove something to a hard-to-please dad.

For decades within the church, dads have been so busy "doing" ministry that they don't have time for their children. Now, an entire generation has thumbed its nose at the church and said, "I don't want it." They're abandoning the church by truckloads.

Why?

Father Power!!!

On the other hand, when father power is used correctly, dads can greatly influence their children's choices, their view of God, the success of their marriages, and their impact on the world. But I'm getting ahead of myself so let's start at the beginning.

In the Beginning

From the beginning of creation, God's plan involved dads. He put the power in **Father Power** because fathers were to be the primary channel for transporting God's Truth to the world. The plan was that dads would pass down everything they knew about God, life, and living to their children, who would then grow up and pass the same information on to their children.

Adam taught his sons about God, creation, Satan, and how he was tossed out of the garden. Adam's sons grew up and taught their sons, who grew up and taught their sons...who taught, Noah, who grew up, got flooded, and taught his sons...get the picture? That was the plan. There just weren't any other options. In fact, writing hadn't even been invented yet.

There was no email, no World Book Encyclopedias, and no Google. Just dads. The only way to transmit information was for a dad to sit down with his children and teach them orally.

There were stories to pass down, genealogies, information about plants and animals, survival skills, getting along with the neighbors, and of course, God's law. It was the law that was first given to a son (Moses) by a father—THE FATHER (Exodus 30, 31).

Upon a fiery mountain, God told Moses everything He wanted him to know about Himself and how His people would relate to Him. Then Moses brought it down from the mountain and read it to the people. Moses didn't have the luxury of zipping over to an Instant Copy and running off a million or so copies of the law to pass out to the people. There was just one copy, and it was kept shut up in the Ark of God.

The plan was for Moses to read the law and for dads and moms to listen, remember it, and then pass it along to their children. We don't know how they did it, but I imagine it was something like this:

A dad and his son were walking along a path to look for some lost sheep, and the boy fell and skinned his knee, letting out some kind of expletive.

His father picked him up, brushed him off, and then let him have it. "Joshua, you know you're never supposed to talk like that. Remember God gave us the command not to use His name in vain..."

Then little Josh would cry (after his spanking) and they'd talk about it some more, along with a host of other things. Then, when the son grew up, he taught it to his son, and so it went, generation after generation.

For a couple of millennium, that's the way it was done. There were no Bibles or copies of the Law. It was written on the hearts of fathers who transferred it to their children by teaching them diligently along life's way.

THE ARCH ENEMY OF FATHER POWER

For a moment, let's pretend you're Satan (nothing personal). Now, if you wanted to interrupt the flow of God's truth, what would you do?

Bingo! You'd go for the source.

It's like planting a new seedling. I used to be in the landscape business, and I've planted thousands of annuals and perennials in my time. I had a technique that was fast and seemed to work well. First, I took the little plastic cell from a flower tray and turned it over. Then, I pushed my thumb or finger up on the bottom of the cell pushing the seedling and it's little ball of artificial dirt and roots out of its container. With my other hand, I grasped the stem of the plant firmly as close to the root as possible, and yanked it from the container.

That was my secret for years, until I happened to watch a gardening show on PBS one Saturday. What the plant expert said rocked my horticulture world. He said that I shouldn't pull the plant out by the stem but by the leaves.

What was he thinking? Why I'd end up pulling half the leaves off if I did it that way. Ahh...but then he went on to give the why behind his statement. The expert explained that if you squeeze the stem too tightly you could damage the whole plant. If you rip off a leaf or two, the plant is still as good as new.

OK, now transfer that to your Satan strategy. If you want to get rid of God's truth, you don't have a bunch of Nazi nuts burn Bibles or ban prayer from school. You don't let Hollywood run amuck and pump sludge into the airwaves. That's just like ripping leaves off the plant. The truth will remain.

If you want to eliminate God's truth, you grab the plant by the stem and give it a good squeeze. And the stem, as far as God's truth is concerned, is the relationship between a father and a son.

Kerplowwy!!!!

Does that blow you away or what? Let me restate the extent of the power that you hold. When God set up the channel through which to transmit His Word, His primary channel was for fathers to tell their sons and daughters. There was no plan B.

In fact, later in Israel's history, there was a time that the people completely ignored God's truth and tossed it aside for some other form of truth...probably cable news (2 Kings 22). Hundreds of years later, while a little repair work was being done on the house of God, some guys stumbled on a copy of the law.

Talk about a surprise. The king read it and found out they were far off the mark. Being a good king, he took steps to correct the great problem that had arisen. Now most Bible scholars will say, "Ah ha!! See that's what happens when you ignore the Bible. The people stuck the text away and that only lead to trouble with a capital T...right there in River City."

But what they fail to realize...is that they're wrong!

The problem was <u>not</u> that scripture was hidden away. The problem...you're way ahead of me on this one...was that fathers weren't doing their jobs of transmitting the truth to their kids. Because the absolute truth is this: if you (being Satan still) were to snap your fingers and cause all the Bibles in the world to disappear, things should go on just as normal.

WHY?

Father power!!!

That's right! Fathers should continue to transmit the truth to their children and they to their children.

Need more evidence?

OK, here it is. Throughout the entire Old Testament we see a continual and gradual abandonment of God's truth. People did what was right in their own eyes. They relied on their own smarts and imitated the wisdom of the world around them. As a result, things got mighty bleak.

Here's the amazing part. Look at the last verse in the Old Testament. It must have been pretty important since it was the last thing mentioned before the coming of the Messiah.

The last verse talks about the front-runner of the messiah. The front-runner was the guy who was supposed to get the rest of the world ready to receive Christ. Without looking, can you guess what the front-runners job was to do?

◆ Pass out tracts warning everyone that He was coming? Nope.

◆ Start a grass roots political committee? No.

♦ Rent out a large facility and hire a caterer? Wrong again.

♦ Visit all the churches inviting them to the "Greet the Messiah Rally on Christmas morning? Not that either.

The job of the front-runner to the Messiah was to turn the hearts of fathers to their children, and the hearts of children to their fathers.

Why?

Father power!!!

The front-runner was to re-establish the channel for the transmission of truth. As it was, the channel was broken. His job was to make it whole again so that when the Messiah came there would be a way to take His message to the world.

And the way the message was to be primarily disseminated was from fathers to son and daughters. Isn't that incredible? The reason it's incredible is because that's the value and importance of the relationship between a father and his children.

That's **Father Power**!

THE BATTLE CONTINUES

Now let's jump back to today. Most would agree that we're far from being a godly nation. We live in a time of school shootings, anything-goes sexuality, gay agendas, pro-abortion, all-time-high divorce rates, and a universal church that is not doing much better.

Conservatives cry out and say it all started when we took prayer out of school. Others say that what we need is better education. The ultra-Biblical right says that we need to put the Bible back in schools and post the Ten Commandments.

While there is some good in all of these solutions, none of them will solve the real problem. These solutions are just the 'leaves' of the problem. Society's problem goes all the way back to the stem. The solution for bringing our society and church back to God is not bringing prayer back into school or posting the ten commandments in court houses...it's not even about using a more effective evangelism program. The solution is to restore the hearts of fathers to their children...or in other words, make being a dad, men's number one priority.

Father Power!

GHOSTS FROM THE PAST

I've got this weird fixation with PBS documentaries. I like to learn about dinosaurs, the civil war, and biographies of famous people. I like to get a behind-the-scene look at some of the famous, and not so famous, names in history.

The common thread in all these people's lives is that they all had fathers. You know what they say, *"If your father didn't have children, chances are neither will you."*

Anyway, it's amazing how deeply affected these famous people were by their fathers. Some had involved, loving fathers, while others had absentee fathers. Some were raised by alcoholics, some by Baptist preachers, and some by war heroes. The effect on each famous person was profound. What each became was primarily based on the influence or lack of influence of their father.

In fact, I just heard a biography on the radio about a racist murderer who is on death row for the murder of an entire family.

Guess what his dad was like? He was a hate-filled, racist, who treated his children harshly and taught them to hate others who were not like them. The man went to a regular school where they taught love and acceptance and walked around in a society that condemned his father's thinking. But one power was greater than the rest and won out.

Father Power.

That's the irony of father power. It's a two-sided sword for good or bad. That's why alcoholics often grew up in alcoholic homes, children of divorced parents are more likely to get divorced, and workaholic dads beget workaholic sons.

GOD IS YOUR ONLY BACK-UP

Want to hear something shocking? You can be replaced as the head of your family! Depressing? Not so, when you consider the rest of the story. Dad, you CAN be replaced as a father and a husband but ONLY by God Himself.

It's the truth; the Bible says so. When a father dies, God has made special provision for the hole he leaves in his family and it isn't a handyman to care for the physical needs of the house or an accountant to take care of the finances. It's not even another father-type figure. God, the heavenly Father, alone fills the dad-shaped vacuum.

The Bible says that He will be a father to the fatherless (Psalm 68:5).

So, in your role as father, only God can replace you.

This is not the case in your job. Any shmoe will do. In fact, if you were to die today, someone would take over your job immediately (probably that friend who's been eyeing your position). Don't believe me? Consider this.

The President of the United States holds the most important job in the world. Yet, if he dies, we have a new president within 24 hours. Boom. Just like that. If you think you're the only one who can do what you do, you're wrong. You can be replaced relatively quickly and **will be** replaced if you disappear.

The job you're enslaved to WILL get done without you. The people you're ministering to at the expense of your family will be ministered to by someone else. The deals that only you can close will happen with or without you.

But if you were to die today, the hole you would leave in your family can only be filled...by God. As far as fathering goes, God is plan B.

Father power.

YOUR ARE GOD TO YOUR CHILDREN

But wait, there's more! Your relationship with your children hugely influences your children's relationship with God. Like it or not, your children view God in the same way they view you.

If they feel secure in your love, they will grow up and feel secure in God's love.

If you are distant and keep them at arm's length, they will assume God does the same. They will have trouble going to Him with their problems because they have trouble going to you.

If they have a dad who is always angry when they spill a glass of milk or when they bump his car, they will grow up thinking that God is easily angered as well. They will walk on eggshells and work to please God, always feeling as though they've let him down.

Ready for this? Guess what an adult believes about God whose earthly father was always gone on business or too busy at the office? He or she believes that God cares very little about his life. He can be reached if something big comes up, but He's uninvolved in the daily aspects of life.

I know people who love God deeply, but have a hard time believing God loves them at all. They try to do all the do's and avoid the don'ts to earn His love. They read their Bible, have devotions, and go to church every time the doors are opened but still spend most of their life feeling defeated.

They read books and try different techniques...but nothing seems to work.

Why?

Father Power.

Sadly, it's hard to change these misconceptions because their fathers have woven them into the very fabric of who they are, stitch by stitch, a little at a time.

On the flip side, if a father communicates love and acceptance, his children will grow up believing God loves them. They will be able to succeed and fail without fear. They will turn to their heavenly Father and trust Him, because they were able to turn to their earthly father and trust him.

They won't struggle with accepting God's love. It will come as naturally as a hug from dad.

Why? Is it because they have a great grasp on their theology and doctrines of God? NO! They will view God in that way because their father taught them to, whether intentionally or not.

That's **Father Power** with a capital P. That's the power you wield. It affects not only your children, but your children's children and their children as well.

How you wield the power will affect the way your great grandchildren view God. Your influence ripples across generations to come. Wow! Awesome! Incredible! And, really, really scary!

A Super Power

Dad, I can't overstate the extent of your power. What your children will one day become is largely dependent on you. What they believe or don't believe about God will come from you. The little words you say or don't say will be cherished or bitterly remembered forever.

Why?

Father Power.

Am I starting to sound like a broken record?

God has laid upon fathers the responsibility of transmitting His truth to the world, one child at a time.

Am I at all diminishing the power of God's written Word? NO! Am I saying that people can't get saved without the aid of another human being? No! What I am saying is that your incredible influence as a dad is the single greatest means of assuring that future generations will follow God. Getting the right men into politics or fighting for religious freedom isn't the key. The key to turning this country around and even the world is through father power.

It's a bit sobering to think that one day our sons and daughters might be sitting around in some small group Bible study and be asked, "What was your relationship with your dad like?"

The room will grow quiet. One by one, our adult children will answer the question. What will they say about our relationship with them? Will they remember a dad who wasn't there, was uninvolved or made promises that were never kept, or will they remember a dad who gave them his time, attention, involvement, and taught them about life, living, and God?

Father Power!

DAD 2 DAD (ON YOUR OWN OR IN A GROUP)

1. Describe your father.

   What kind of relationship do you have or did you have with your father?

   If you could change one thing about your relationship with him, what would that be?

2. What do you do that your father did...both good and bad?

3. In a few words, how do you think your children would describe you? (If you're brave, ask them to describe you.)

4. How do you view God? (Ex: loving, standoffish, angry, stern, dependable)

5. How do you think your children view God? (Again, if you really want a clear answer, ask your children to answer the question.)

6. How would you say you're doing in transmitting God's truth to your children?

WITH GREAT POWER COMES GREAT RESPONSIBILITY—PART 1

A few years ago on a lazy New Year's night, I saw part of the first Spiderman movie on TV. I'm not sure about all the details, but Peter Parker (AKA Spiderman) was struggling with this amazing superhero ability that had been thrust upon him. He was talking to his Uncle (I think) who had been a huge influence in his life, and his uncle offered this warning, "*With great power comes great responsibility.*"

You know what? That bit of wisdom applies not only to spider power but to **Father Power** as well.

So what are you supposed to do with all this power you have? The question you need to ask is what would Jesus have YOU do with that power? Now any Baptist worth his salt will immediately ask what the Bible has to say concerning that.

So, let's see what the Bible has to say specifically to dads. That is pretty important right? It's the secret weapon that instructs us how to use our power.

The word 'father' appears 396 times in the Bible, but you can eliminate most of these references because they refer to our ancestors (forefathers). Then if you remove the verses that describe a condition (a wise father...) rather than give an instruction, you have only two left.

Out of the entire Bible, there are only two verses that give specific instructions to fathers and they are almost identical.

One verse is in the letter to the Ephesians and the other is in the letter to the Colossians. The Apostle Paul wrote both letters, and both letters were written to a bunch of dads just like you.

For our purposes, we're going to spend most of our time looking at the letter to the Ephesian dads.

DADS ARE DADS

Try to think of the letter to the Ephesian dads as...well, a letter or maybe an email written from one friend to another. Paul was encouraging the church in the areas in which they had been struggling. He addressed husbands, wives, and children, and then he directed one sentence to the dads in the crowd.

"And Fathers..."

Every dad was quiet waiting to hear what Paul had to say.

"And Fathers, do not provoke your children to anger..."

Now, before we proceed it should be noted that when you're reading a letter from the Bible, it is a two-way street. It's kind of like listening to your wife on the telephone. It doesn't take much eavesdropping before you know exactly whom she's talking to, what they are talking about, and why they're talking about what they're talking about. You get that information from what your wife says and how she says it.

The same is true with a letter in scripture. We can infer a lot about what was going on from the topics addressed.

For example, if Paul wrote about how to get along with others, we can assume people weren't getting along or if he told them to stand strong under persecution, we can safely assume that the readers were facing persecution.

So, when Paul says, "Fathers do not provoke your children to anger," we can very safely assume that the dads were provoking their children to anger. In fact, a more accurate rendering of the text is, "Fathers, STOP provoking your children to anger."

I take comfort in knowing that 2000 years ago dads were muffing it just like I do today. Instead of getting all bent out of shape because the kids left their toys in the driveway, they probably got mad because the kids left their toys in front of the chariot.

I hope that's comforting to you too, dad. Not much has changed in the last couple of millennia. Kids are kids, and dads don't always handle it well. The same is true with the families around you.

We tend to think that the dads around us don't struggle with being a good dad. Or we watch some parenting expert on a video and think, "He has it all together." You might even be tempted to think that I have it all together. After all, I am *The Familyman*.

Well, in case you are thinking that—you're dead wrong. Just to prove it, I'll give you my telephone number, and you can call and ask my wife how often I blow it. 574-65...on the other hand, maybe I won't.

Anyway...we all blow it.

THE DARK SIDE OF FATHER POWER

Provoking children to anger is the dark side of father power. It is a terribly destructive force that we dads wield and hold over our children. 'Provoking to anger' is the act of withholding something from our children that they need.

Make sense? I didn't think so either.

Maybe this story will help. Several years ago, when I was a strapping, young lad, newly married, and good looking as all get out, I took my lovely bride to a small park on the outskirts of town in Northern Indiana.

We were resting in the shade of a clump of maple trees when a loud car pulled up and a seedy looking guy in a white T-shirt with a bandanna on his head stepped from the car. He looked around and then opened the back door and pulled out a large boat anchor chain that was obviously attached to an animal of some kind. I assumed it was a tiger or a Kodiak bear based on the thickness of the chain.

Instead, a muscular pit bull with a nail-studded collar leaped out from the back seat. I felt pretty safe since he was on a chain, and I had me wife to protect me, so I sat there watching the guy and his dog.

After a few minutes, it was obvious that the guy wasn't there to leisurely stroll through the park with his dog. He was there to show off. From somewhere, he pulled out a big old leg bone...I assumed it was from an animal and not a murder victim...and he held it up for the dog to examine.

The pit bull went wild and lunged at the bone, but Mr. Bandanna Guy pulled the bone out of his reach just as he was about to clamp down on it. Then he walked up to a tree and held the bone high against the trunk. The dog scraped at the bark trying to get to the bone. He'd get pretty high, but the guy always kept the bone just out of his reach. Over and over, he taunted the dog, always pulling the bone away just as the dog was about to get it.

The pit bull growled and was mad as a hornet. I half wondered when the dog would give up on the bone and go for the nice, juicy arm bone of bandanna guy instead. I even decided that I'd take my time coming to his rescue.

But here's the point: the bandanna guy was provoking his dog to anger. He was withholding something that the dog desperately wanted...always keeping it just out of reach.

Sometimes we do that to our children.

THE NEEDS OF OUR CHILDREN

Let me ask you a question. What do your children need from you? What are the things you provide them with that will ensure that they become happy, well-adjusted adults who have successful marriages, families, and lives? When I speak to groups of dads, I ask them these same questions. It takes them a few minutes to get rolling (they are men after all), but eventually they begin to shout out different answers. I've included some of them:

Time

Affection

Someone who will listen to them

Approval

Discipline

Protection

Unconditional love

Unconditional like

Fun

This list isn't complete, but it's a good start. These are the tools that put the Power in Father Power. When used correctly, you assure your children's success. If used incorrectly, you can do great damage that only God can repair. Now, let's spend the rest of this chapter and the next one looking at each of these tools.

NEED: TIME

I don't know how many times I've heard the debate about quality time versus quantity time. Both sides seem to have convincing arguments, and if you listen long enough, you can find someone who will back up what you already do...or don't do.

We're going to toss aside the semantics and simply state that kids need both quantity time and quality time. Your kids need lots of time where you're just "there" as well as time where you're doing something purposefully together.

QUANTITY TIME

Quantity time means, "being there" time. As soon as I come home from work, I walk in the door and look for my wife. I quietly tiptoe around to find her and then I sit down on the couch with her to talk about the day.

Apparently, my kids have some kind of built-in-dad sensor because minutes later, they gallop down the steps and surround my wife and I.

I greet the kids and then discreetly motion to my wife and ask her to meet me in the next room so we can try to resume our talking in silence...or semi-silence.

Moments later, we are surrounded once again in our new location, and I look at my wife and holler, "Can't they play somewhere else?"

She smiles understandingly and answers, "They just want to be near us."

But that's not the end of it. They follow me everywhere.

When I sneak out into the garage to work on a project, the next thing I know one of the kids is standing beside me looking at me.

"What's up?" I ask, expecting a reasonable explanation for his ruining my 'quiet time.'

"Nothing," he says with a winning smile, "I just wondered what you are doing out here."

I answer him hoping that now that he knows the answer he'll go back inside. But instead of leaving, he decides to start his own project. Ten minutes later, all my kids are outside pounding nails, sawing boards, and making messes.

Even when I go inside to get something, one of the kids looks up and asks, "Where are you going?"

"I'm going inside to get something," I say disgustedly.

"Are you coming back," he asks.

"Yes, I'll be right back."

"Soon?"

"YES! I'll be back in a few minutes!" I say.

Now if I were him, I wouldn't want someone as mean and grumpy as me coming back, but he's satisfied with my answer and returns to whatever he's doing, glad that I'm coming back.

Now, let me ask you: why did he want me to be in the garage with him? I wasn't doing anything with him. We weren't having some deep meaningful conversation where he could ask questions and I could fill his tank with all kinds of fatherly wisdom.

The answer: Quantity time—he just wanted to be near me. Nothing more.

The moral of the story is your kids want you to be around. They want you to be in the same house, in the same yard, and sometimes to your chagrin, in the same square foot. Why? Because there is safety in knowing that dad is close-by.

Your kids want you to be at the dinner table, at bedtime prayers, at ballgames, and at video nights. You don't always need to be doing something super fatherly, but you do need to be around. And the truth is you can't be around if...uh...you're not around.

When you're on the road staying in some hotel, you are not around. When you're working late into the night, you are not around. When you get up early so you can get a jump on your workday, you are not around. When you are playing golf, bowling with the guys, or playing ball down at the gym, you are not around.

"Well," you argue, "I can't just quit my job and bum around home all the time."

True, but let's get something straight. First of all, I'm not talking about quitting your job and sitting around home all day long. I'm talking about 'being around.' Secondly, I'm merely laying out our children's needs right now; we'll talk about a course of action later.

So let me state it again: Your children need you around, lots. When you're not around, you provoke them to anger.

QUALITY TIME

The key to quality time is what you do during quantity time. The truth is, any dad can get straight A's in quantity time...a table lamp can do that much. The tougher of the two is quality time.

Quality time is giving your children the best of your time, not just the leftover time. We dads have a hard time with this one...let me restate that, THIS dad has a hard time with this one.

See, I'm all for quantity time. In fact, I can get all kinds of stuff done when I'm just "around." I can work on garage projects, work on the computer, and even watch an occasional PBS documentary, because I'm AROUND.

It's when we're working out in the garage and they say something like, "Dad, can we build a rubber band gun out of wood?" that the real test comes.

All of sudden, it goes from 'it's nice having you around dad'...to 'Dad, can you stop doing what you think is important and do what I think is important.'

That's the crux of quality time. You have to stop doing what's important to you and do what's important to them...and sometimes what's important to them doesn't seem very important.

So, I'm asking you, is it important for me to build a rubber band gun? Is it important to show my son how to draw on the computer or set up the train, look at his newest Lego creation or read him a story about a lion, or play another round of the game Hi-Ho Cheerio?

It may not seem important to me...BUT it is important to them. They remind me of it too with comments like, "You never do what I want to do."

Now I could say, "That's not true!" but the truth is...that is true.

Quality time demands that I give my children the best of my time, which just so happens to be the most inconvenient time.

Even as I type this, my seven-year-old daughter has stepped into my office and wants to know if I'll go get her some pie filling so she can bake a dessert. Now, I don't want to stop what I'm doing, drive to the store to pick up a can of blueberry glop that probably won't even be edible when it's finished...but it's important to my daughter...so I need to make it important to me.

"So what you're saying is that I have to do everything my kids ask me to do? If my son calls me at work and wants me to come home and read him a book, I have to do that?" you might ask.

Of course I'm not saying that. But I am saying you have to give them your best time. My daughter has asked me to do something that is within my power to grant. It will mean I'll have to give up some of my time to meet her needs. That's quality.

The next few paragraphs all fit under this umbrella of quality time. There are additional tools needed like affection, listening, and approval, but the most important thing to remember is to give them your best time.

It means playing games, riding bikes, playing catch, camping in a tent in the backyard, catching lighting bugs, going shopping, watching stars, stopping for ice cream, reading books aloud, working on a project together, and saying prayers before bed.

By giving them quality time, you prove to them that they are important to you. When you withhold quality time and miss those opportunities for whatever reason, you convey to your children that they are low on your priority list, AND you provoke your children to anger.

Note: I've got to take a break now, dad, and go get the blue-berry glop for my princess.

Here's a list of some "quality time" activities that you can do with your children. Try to do at least one this weekend:

√ Bowling
√ Skating
√ Wash a car together
√ Play a child's favorite board game
√ Play a child's favorite video game
√ Take a child out to lunch
√ Go for a bike ride
√ Work on a project together
√ Do something you've been promising for a long time
√ A backyard campout
√ A canoe trip
√ A father/daughter tea party
√ Take a daughter to the mall
√ Read a book out loud
√ Spend 15 minutes talking and tucking a child into bed
√ Go fishing
√ Brush your daughter's hair

NEED: AFFECTION

There are hugging families and there are non-hugging families. I was raised in a non-hugging one. My mom hugged and kissed us...that's expected, but the rest of us didn't really touch much unless it was a good slug in the arm or something.

Regardless of your upbringing, every child needs to be loved, hugged, and touched. I worked for years as a pastor. I especially liked working with the pre-teens. I was involved in kids' outreach events, Bible clubs, and mid-week kids' clubs.

What amazed me the most was the number of kids who barely knew me and yet came up and hugged me like I was their best friend. It was usually the same kids each week. As soon as the night started, they'd greet me with a hug, and before they left, I got another hug.

It was obvious they didn't get much hugging at home and needed to fill up their tanks while they were at church. I determined then that I would fill up my kids' tanks at home so they wouldn't need to look elsewhere.

Studies have shown that girls are especially needy of a father's touch. Those who go without it often look for boys to fill that need. Studies also reveal that homosexual men often got very little affection from their fathers.

Isn't it amazing that a son who is not given the love and affection that he needs from his father can fall into a destructive, sinful lifestyle? Why? You know the answer.

Father Power.

Some of your children need an extra amount of touching.

Sam, my second oldest, loves to be close...I mean real close. When walking together, he holds my hand and then places my hand on top of his head and then entangles his arms around my waist. He loves it. It makes him feel close...it makes me feel like I'm walking with an octopus. I know he needs it so I tolerate it...and sometimes even find myself enjoying it.

I work hard to touch my children. They don't have to work at it. It comes natural to them. They want to touch me. I have to fight the urge to push them away. My oldest son, Ben, will still walk around a crowded hall holding my hand.

Now, I don't know about you, but guys didn't hold each other's hand like this when I was growing up in America— the land of the red-blooded male.

And when my son grabs my hand out in public, I still feel a little awkward. So you know what I do?

I HOLD HIS HAND.

He needs my touch, and I'm going to give it to him as long as he wants it and even when he thinks he doesn't want it. And I'm trying to ensure he'll want it forever. That's why I kiss him, hug him, and squeeze him. I cuddle with him on our big bear chair and let him bruise my body with his bony knees and elbows.

All dads are not "touchers" by nature, but they better be doing it because their kids need it. Your kids need it. Your daughters need you to hold them and your sons need you to touch them. If you do, they'll come back for more and more. They won't go somewhere else looking for it. Your touch means security and reassurance that you love them.

Your lack of touch provokes them to anger.

Father Power.

NEED: LISTENING

Children need dads who listen to them as much as wives need husbands to listen to them.

I learned an important lesson about listening not long ago. I learned it from observing my wife and youngest son, Abe. I was in the kitchen while my wife was at the computer typing away frantically.

Click-click-clickity click...away she typed like the wind. Abe walked in and wanted her attention.

"Mom. Mom. Mom..."

"What is it honey?" she said still typing away.

"Mom. Mom. Mom..."

Without missing a key stroke, my wife said, "Abe, I'm listening. What do you want?"

The clicking continued and so did Abe.

"Mom, Mom. Mom. Mom..."

"What is it?! She asked a little louder but still typing away.

"Mom. Mom. Mom..."

Finally the clicking stopped. She turned and looked Abe in the eye, and asked, "What do you want, Abe?"

Abe immediately asked his pressing question because NOW his mother was listening.

Dad, that's what our children want and need. They want us to stop doing what we're doing, look them in the eye, listen, and respond thoughtfully.

I have one son who is a 'describer.' He goes into great detail to describe his latest Lego creation. He holds the little plastic ship up to my eye and then tells me the function of each little piece. Honestly, I have trouble focusing. I find myself nodding and saying, "Uh, huh, yeah, yeah...neat."

"You're not listening," he accuses me. It's true, but I try to act like I am. The problem is that I don't care about Lego boats and the million details that go along with them.

What I convey to my son is that I don't care about him.

To show him I care, I have to work hard at focusing my mind not only on what he is showing me but also on him. Sometimes that means I have to turn away from my computer, turn off the TV, put down my project, or turn the saw off and look him in the eyes.

Ooooh, I hit a nerve, didn't I? Do your kids come up to you and want your attention right in the middle of a big game or while you're on-line? You know what you need to do...

"Yeah, but the game is important!!!" you argue.

No. Ballgames are FUN to watch...your kids are important.

Here's a little test: Do you ever hear the phrase, "You never listen to me," come out of your child's sweet little mouth? If the answer is yes, don't brush it off by saying they're exaggerating. Instead, let those phrases act like little red flags because when your children say that, it's because they feel that. You know what? I'm guilty.

When we don't listen, we provoke our kids to anger.

Father power.

Have you ever noticed that we dads are solvers? On those rare occasions when our children invite us into their private world to tell us something important, we try to solve it and offer all our fatherly wisdom and immediately the door to the private world is shut, locked, and we're not invited in again.

So when your daughter says she thinks 'Josh' is really handsome, don't say, "You're too young to be thinking about boys...that's silly...go wash some dishes!" Instead, smile, nod your head, and pray with her about which man God would choose for her.

When your son is worried about the future, don't brush it off—listen.

You have to be there though for them to talk with you. If you're not there, they can't talk. I know the miracle of cell phones, but it's not the same as talking to your child in a little fishing boat, on the edge of bed at the end of the day, or talking over ice cream on a summer's night.

Dad, your children will love you if you listen to them rattle, rant, describe, dream, and whisper their thoughts to you. If you don't, they'll find someone else to listen...and you don't want that. You want to be the person that they come to when they need to talk about important stuff or Lego stuff.

It's not really that hard to do. All you have to do is lead them to the 'talking places'—the places where hearts are opened and kids talk. You don't have to prod them or have some plan of getting to the root of the conversation. In fact, you won't have to do a single thing except wait for them to make the first move.

The car is one of the best talking places. There's just something about two people alone in the car that brings out good conversation. When I take a kid along on an errand, we've covered half a dozen topics...none of which are deep, before we're even out of the driveway. Then, somewhere along the way, we move into deeper conversation.

I listen, I mean really listen, and do my best to offer thoughtful answers. But it's not always easy. Just a few weeks ago, I had a speaking engagement three hours away. I decided it would be a good thing to take my son Sam along for the ride.

We sang, made silly faces, and were goofy most of the way there. I think the deepest thing we talked about was how when it rains, it makes you want to go to the bathroom. It wasn't easy. There were times I just wanted to tune him out, nod my head, and say, "Uh huh," without really listening.

In fact, it would have been easier to travel by myself. It always is. But when we travel or run errands alone, we miss out on giving our children something they need...time talking with dad.

Why is listening to our children so important???

Father Power!

My friend Ken Pierpont drew up this set of questions that can be asked to your child when you have some alone time (like on a birthday breakfast to McDonald's). The questions are meant to help you get the conversation started. Now this might seem a little awkward so he suggests that you just say, "Hey, I've got these questions and I know it seems dumb...but would you just humor me and answer the questions. Who knows maybe it won't be so bad." So here's the first question..."

1. What foods do you like and dislike the most?
2. Who is your best friend? What makes him/her your best friend?

3. Who do you want to be most like when you grow up?
4. What embarrasses you most in our family relationships?
5. What is the greatest fear in your life?
6. What is your favorite activity?
7. What is your favorite song? Favorite kind of music?
8. What do you like to learn about the most?
9. What accomplishments in your life so far give you the greatest sense of achievement?
10. What irritations in our family bother you the most?
11. What really makes you angry?
12. What do you want to do when you grow up?
13. What has been the biggest disappointment in your life so far?
14. If you could change anything about the way you look, what would you change?
15. What do you appreciate most about each member of our family?
16. What do you like to do most as a family?
17. Be honest. If you could change anything about me, what would you change?

NEED: APPROVAL

The story is told that a successful businessman was honored at a university graduation for his success and achievement. The crowd applauded as the man took the podium to address the people. Oddly, He looked up towards the ceiling and said, "Is this good enough for you dad?"

It was sad, but apparently the man never got the approval of his father. He built a monstrous corporation and made billions, but it was never good enough.

Later, I heard the same businessman's father tell a re-
porter that the way to assure your children will be great is to
keep them insecure. Don't let them ever think they've done
a good job...otherwise they'll quit trying. Instead, withhold
(there's that word) praise, and they'll keep seeking to do
better."

Well, from one dad to another, let me just say, "THAT'S
THE DUMBEST THING I'VE EVER HEARD!!!!!

Children need our praise and approval as much as they
need air and water. A child who feels his father's approval
will be forever secure in his love. And not only that, he will
feel secure in God's love.

On the other hand, a child who is always trying to win
his father's approval will forever be trying to win God's approval.

Maybe you didn't have a father who praised you and so
it's hard for you to praise your children. For the sake of your
children, it's time to change.

Every kid needs to feel 'liked,' not for what he achieves
but for who he is. I know some people who as children only
felt liked when they did well. If they got good grades, scored
a goal, or did well, they were praised and were more liked
than if they didn't.

Let me brag about my dad for a minute. He was and is a
great dad. He didn't care if I struck out a dozen times (which
I often did), got all C's on my report card, or was cut from
the team. He told me I was great, and he did the same for my
brother's and sister, who were a lot worse than I.

I remember coming home one time from school with
straight A's on my report card. I ran in, stuffed it into the

hands of my dad and waited for his surprise. Know what he said?

"That's great Todd, but would your teacher say you are the nicest?"

What he taught me right then and which I've never forgotten, was that his approval wasn't based on how smart I was or am. He was more concerned about how nice I was. As a result, I've grown up to be a nice guy...dumber than a sack of turnips, but nice.

I know other children who brought all A's and one B home on their report card, and you know what their dad said?

"Let's see if you can bring that B up to an A."

You tell me, what does that convey to a child? It says, "I'd like you better if you got all A's." Did that father mean to convey that—probably not, but that's what was perceived.

I work hard at my house to make sure my children know they are loved for who they are and not for what they do or how they perform. When my kids were little, we played a game about how much I loved them.

It always started like this:

"I love you, Sam."

"Even if I do bad things?"

"Yep, even if you do bad things."

"What if I do really, really bad things?"

"Even if you do really, really, really bad things, I'll still love you."

"What...if I kill someone?" He is smiling ear to ear because he knows the answer.

"Even if you kill someone, I'll still love you...but don't kill anyone."

You tell me what effect that has on my child? What effect would it have on your child to know that his dad loves him and likes him know matter how he performs?

Is it easy? No. I blow it continually.

I remember one Sunday in particular. I was a pastor at a small church and there was pressure to look like we had the perfect family...you know, obedient children, a smiling wife, and a spiritual husband.

Well, that day one of my children acted terribly. He was throwing some kind of fit for the entire world to see, and I was ready to throttle him. Of course, I didn't look that way. I was the perfect picture of calm and godliness as I sauntered over to where the 'boy' stood.

I leaned over in his face, grabbed his little arm and hissed, "Stop it right now, you're embarrassing me."

I'll never forget the look in his eyes that said, "You don't like me, do you dad?" I hated that look, and right then I decided that never again would I turn against my children.

Now when one throws a fit, I wrap my arm around him and say, "That's my boy!" Later, I spank him and have 'the talk,' but in public I stand beside him.

The need for affirmation doesn't change when children grow up either. Another time when I was a pastor, a young lady was brought before the church because she was pregnant and unmarried.

The girl was crying as the pastor explained the situation. Most people kept their heads down in shame and awkwardness, but not her dad. He stood beside her straight as an arrow. His head was held high and he scanned the room like he was looking for anyone who might need a little attitude adjustment.

Was he embarrassed? Oh yeah. Was he disappointed with his daughter's choices? Yes. But there was no doubt in my mind or his daughter's that her dad loved her. That's what I want for my children and that's what God wants for yours.

Father Power!

Approval doesn't come naturally. Approval only happens because a dad determines to give it. You must decide to cheer when they win and cheer even louder when they fail. Throw your arms around your child for no apparent reason and say, "I think you're great. I'm the luckiest dad in the world to have you as my son...boy, you handled that well...you are growing up to be a wonderful young lady...I love you."

When we withhold our approval or make our children earn it, we provoke them to anger.

DAD 2 DAD (ON YOUR OWN OR IN A GROUP)

1. Which is easier for you to give: quantity time or quality time?

   Which of the two do your children seem to need the most of from you?

2. Is it easy or hard for you to be affectionate with your children?

   Why do you think that is?

3. Do you think you are a good listener?

   What would make you a better listener?

4. Is it easy for you to give approval to your children?

   Did your father give his approval easily?

With Great Power Comes Great Responsibility–Part 2

Need: Discipline

Did you know that your children want you to discipline them? In fact, they need you to discipline them. There's comfort and security in knowing that there are consequences when they've crossed the limits set by you.

As a father, you begin to discipline your child when he starts crawling. He makes his way to a wall socket and you gently remove him from danger. Being a normal child, he looks at you and then at the wall socket and scoots as quickly as his little knees will carry him right back to the socket.

Now, with a little more firmness, you tell him "No" and pick him up and cart him to another room. Now, repeat that scenario several more times and the child finally realizes he's not allowed to touch the wall socket.

You go through the inconvenience of keeping a little kid away from the wall socket because you love him and care about his life and future. That's why you set certain standards for your children and go through all the hassle of making sure they keep the standards. That's why you discipline your children for not keeping the standard. You love them and it's one of the ways you prove it to them daily.

Matter of fact, my wife just called me upstairs twenty minutes ago to deal with one of my sons who had whacked his brother on the head with a blunt object. I didn't want to go upstairs and deal with him. I wanted to continue typing away on my computer telling YOU how to deal with your kids. I knew it would interrupt my momentum and would take longer than I wanted it to take. BUT I was the dad, and I knew it was my job to deal with it.

I was right. It did interrupt the zone I was in. It did take a while to talk about the situation, tell him what was expected of him, paddle him, and make sure he felt loved and restored afterwards.

It would have been much easier to say, "Can't right now Honey...maybe later."

Had I done that and stayed in my office, I would have provoked my son to anger. Instead, I conveyed to my son, by taking the time to discipline him that I care about how he behaves and I care even more about him. He didn't thank me for warming up his back end...but one day he will.

Discipline is not just a little kid thing; it's also a big kid thing. Children of all ages need their dads to stand their ground and hold them to the line.

A few years ago, Steven Spielberg produced the based-on-a-true-story-movie, "Catch Me if You Can." It starred Tom Hanks as an FBI agent who was determined to catch a check-forging teenager played by Leonardo DiCaprio.

It was a fascinating story about a seventeen-year-old boy who impersonated an airline pilot, a doctor, and an attorney. And as if that wasn't enough, he also forged and cashed over four million dollars worth of fake checks...all before the age of nineteen.

At some point in the movie, DiCaprio met his dad (who was also skirting the law) in a dark, neighborhood bar. His father, impressed by his son's clever antics, encouraged him to keep running. The son questioned his dad.

"I'm your father," he answered with authority.

The boy, who was tired of the deadly game, leaned into his father's face and pleaded, "Then tell me to stop!"

His father didn't, and the boy walked away disappointed.

Dad, although parenting a teenager isn't the same as parenting an eight-year-old, a teenager still wants his dad to say, "Stop." He may not act like it, but he will respect you for it.

Your son needs you to set a curfew and to enforce it. He needs you to ask him tough questions, and to protect him from intimate relationships with the opposite sex. That means you'll have to say, "You can't always be with your girlfriend...you can't be alone at her house or in the car...or in the same STATE!! (Sorry, I overreacted).

Your teenage daughter needs you to tell her when she's dressed immodestly or is flirtatious around boys. She needs you to send her back to her room to get some clothes on that cover her body. That's your job. Your teenagers may kick and scream and call you unfair, but deep down they want you to hold them to the line. They will respect you for disciplining them when they cross the line.

Like the son in the movie demonstrated, when we don't discipline our children, we provoke them to anger.

Need: Protection

One spring, we visited St. Augustine, Florida (the oldest city in America). We toured the Castillo de San Marcos (an old fort), walked the 219 steps to the top of a big black-and-white striped lighthouse, and even managed to spend a couple of hours at the beach. Oh, and I had time to rip the taillight off, and put a gash in the fender of, a brand new Mercedes.

The beach was beautiful, although there was a big sign warning how the rip tide could suck you or your children out into the middle of the ocean. No big deal for the average swimmer, but this dad takes the ocean, rip tides, and signs that read, "No lifeguard on duty—swim at your own risk" very seriously.

I've always been a little scared of the ocean, and when my kids are in the water, I'm on them like a tick on a hound dog. They played while I watched, standing in the surf and ready to jump into action if needed. I didn't care what the signs said—THIS DAD IS ON DUTY, I thought. I am my children's lifeguard. Other children may be up to their heads in dangerous surf but not mine.

A few days later, I was reminded that my lifeguarding involves more than just beach duty; it involves most areas of their young lives. We pulled into a parking lot and stood face-to-face with a trailer plastered with a half-naked young lady selling something.

My son noticed. In the past, he wouldn't have, but now he's older, and he NOTICED.

I thought it over for the next 800 miles of RVing and knew what I needed to do. I'm the lifeguard, and I'm on duty. I can't keep them from seeing everything, but I can do a lot to keep them from seeing MOST of it. I can show them how to look away, warn them of the danger spots, and tell them what happens if they don't turn away (Proverbs 7).

Never before have our children and families been so bombarded by sensual images on videos, billboards, checkout stands, television shows and commercials, and video games. Status quo says, "That's just the way it is...you can't hide in a cave."

Father Power says, "Not on my shift...I'm on duty."

So we dads need to know what our children are watching, reading, and playing. I know it's a huge pain to have to preview every movie, book, and video game. It's not always popular to say, "No you can't read that book...no, you can't watch that movie...or no, you can't play that video." But that's our job...in fact, it's your job.

These immodest images are like rip tides; they lead to deep water where men die.

How about you, Dad? Have you let your guard down? Your kids are counting on you to keep them away from the rip tides of life. Do what you have to do. Don't listen to their pleas that say, *"That's not fair."* After all, you 'da lifeguard and you're on duty!

Need: Unconditional Love

If you've spent much time in church then you are well acquainted with the term 'unconditional love.' It's the kind of love that God has for us. It is not based on any conditions. Unconditional love says, "You may treat me like dirt, turn your back on me, and be unresponsive to my gifts of love, but I still love you...and I will continue to show you that love even though you act like a jerk."

Sound good? You bet. I'd love for my wife to show me that kind of love...and I know she'd like that kind of love from me.

In a world in which good performance is rewarded and poor performance is punished, unconditional love seems unheard of. Why would you reward those who fail, sin, or spurn the love you try to show them? An eye for an eye...a tooth for a tooth—that's the American way.

But that's not THE Father's way and it's not a father's way. As a dad, your duty is to love your children unconditionally. That simply means that you love your children in such a way that it is not dependent on their performance. It should be a flat line on the love-o-meter indicator.

Remember the "I love you" game I mentioned a few pages ago? It's real easy to say I love you in the hypothetical realm but it's much more difficult to demonstrate love to a child who has made unwise choices, fails a class, gets in a fight, says ugly, hateful things to you or your wife, walks away from everything you hold dear, or just makes a lot of messes.

But if we only give love when our children act lovable, we're just rewarding their behavior and it's not much different than giving a fish to the seal who jumps through the hoop at Sea World.

As important as it is to demonstrate (or prove by your actions) unconditional love, it's just as important to verbally remind your children, as well as your wife, that without a doubt, you love them more than anything.

HAVE I TOLD YOU LATELY THAT I LOVE YOU?

Is it hard for you to say, "I love you" to the people you love the most? Maybe you were raised in a family that didn't verbally express love. There have certainly been eras in which fathers didn't say, "I love you" to their children.

I love the musical "Fiddler on the Roof." What's not to love about big, brash, and loud Revtevia, the patriarch of the family? One of my favorite moments in the movie is when Revtevia asks his wife in song, "Do you love me?"

She immediately begins to describe all the things she does for him...like washing his clothes, ironing his shirts, and cooking his meals.

Not satisfied, he asks, "Yes, but do you love me?"

Again, she talks about bearing his children and other things she has done for him.

Finally he says, "Yes, BUT DO YOU LOVE ME?"

In his deep bass voice he is telling his wife, "Yes, I know you've acted loving...but I want to hear the words."

Your children need to hear the words from your mouth as well.

A Sad Story

Denise Rainey tells this story regarding the power of a father verbally saying "I love you."

"A young woman I heard about was so desperate to reach out to her unfeeling father that she got herself arrested for shoplifting. That didn't work, so she decided to stop eating. She developed anorexia, and later, a brain tumor that the doctors said she caused in part by her undernourished condition.

"I was lying in my hospital bed near death with all kinds of tubes coming out of my body when my father finally came to see me," the woman recalled. "We talked for about an hour; then he got up to leave. As he opened my hospital door, I guess I just went berserk. I began to scream, 'You just can't say it, can you?'" She screamed even louder, "I'm going to die, and you still can't say it!"

Her father said, "Say what?"

"I love you," she said.

He finally broke down and began to weep. He moved to her bedside and through his tears said those words the young woman needed to hear so desperately." *(Taken from Men of Integrity - March/April, Saturday, April 3)*

That's Father Power...and the power of the words, "I love you."

Dad, your children need to hear the words "I love you" from your lips. It's not good enough to show it and assume they know you love them. They need to hear it...often. How often? Every day.

Say it when you get up, when you leave for work, and at bedtime. Say it for no apparent reason and after your child has done something wrong or disobeyed. Little boys and girls and grown-up boys and girls need to hear over and over, "Dad loves you." Why?

Father Power.

Need: Unconditional like

Unconditional like is the SMILE in unconditional love. Unconditional love says I love you no matter what. It's like a non-negotiable contract that states that dads have to love their kids...it's the law.

Unconditional like is not about laws; it bubbles up in the heart. It says that when I have to choose teams I want you on my team because I think you're the best. That's where the smile comes in, because when you smile at your child you communicate unconditional like.

Even the smallest child knows that when you smile at them you are pleased with them. Now let me ask you a question: when was the last time you smiled at your children?

Maybe it's been too long, because they don't give you much to smile about. It seems like every time you talk with them you're correcting them.

Don't hit your brother...

Don't leave that in the car...

Clean up this room...

When are you ever going to take responsibility...?

How many times do I have to tell you...?

Do you have to whine about everything...?

Sit up straight...

Get a haircut...

Be nice...

Stop doing that...

Sound familiar? Man, sometimes I spend so much time correcting that I forget to smile. When I don't smile, I communicate that I don't LIKE my children and they feel like I don't like them. Their faces reflect it...because they don't smile either.

The truth is: a smiley child receives a lot of smiles and a smiley child feels liked.

Now let me ask you: do your children smile?

If not, then try really hard to smile at your kids. When they pester you...smile. When they interrupt you...smile. When their room looks like a pit, tell them to clean it up...but smile. When they disobey you, correct them...and then smile at them. You'll be amazed at the difference.

A smile is the key to unconditional like.

NEED: FUN

When was the last time you just had fun with your kids? I don't mean when did you last work on a project or clean out the garage, but when did you last do something just for the fun of it like playing tag, having a snowball fight, or having a pillow fight before bed?

Some of my fondest memories are the times when my dad played with my brothers and sister and me. Although it was fun to play at our lake cottage in the water with my brothers, sister, and cousins, it was way cooler when my dad whipped off his shirt and joined us.

I know my kids like it too. I can tell because they ask me to do things with them all the time.

"Dad, can you come out and jump on the trampoline with us? Dad, can you play flashlight tag with us tonight? Dad, can you play Battleship with me?"

The problem is that to do **their things**, I have to stop doing **my things** and get hot, tired, or rumpled.

But I know my children need to have fun with me. If I'm all about business, and I just don't have time for fun with my children, then I provoke them to anger.

You know why...**Father Power**.

Having fun with your children is as easy as saying...sure. I learned this at my in-law's lake cottage one 4th of July. It had been a great weekend—eating lots of good food, playing out in the sun with my family, and enjoying the rocket's red glare and the bombs bursting in mid-air. The only bad part of the weekend was the odd feeling that came over me early on the morning of the fourth.

The sun was shining, the sky was as blue as can be, and the water felt warm. I was basking in the sun when I noticed something...disturbing.

One of my nephews ran up to Alan, my brother-in-law, and asked, "Dad, can I go skiing?"

"Sure," he answered cheerfully...a little too cheerfully for my liking. He walked down the long pier, uncovered the boat, gathered the skis and life jackets, untangled the rope, and THEN took them skiing.

I would have said, "How about tomorrow?"

Later that night, one of the older kids asked Alan, "Dad, can we help light some of the fireworks?"

I knew they were way too young for something like that, so I was flabbergasted when he said, "Sure."

I would have responded, "Maybe next year."

While watching their fireworks display, a feeling of 'dad-envy' crept over me.

The next morning Alan said "Sure," again to a boat ride, skiing, AND fishing.

By the last day, I had discovered one of Alan's secrets to good fathering—he says, "Sure," a lot.

Fifteen minutes later, my chance came to try out my theory.

I was on the front porch enjoying the shade when my son Ike asked for a Jet Ski ride. "Sure," I said, pleased with my convincing tone.

Then later that day Alan asked, "You want to go 'tubing' with the kids and me?

"Sure," I said.

I was glad I did—and so were my kids.

I realized that weekend that maybe it's time for us dads to say, "Sure" more often. When your son asks you to shoot some hoops say, "Sure." When your daughter wants to talk about her future say, "Sure." When your wife asks you to fix the broken screen, answer, "Sure!"

You may not feel like saying it, but say it anyway. No excuses; just say, "Sure."

Try it out for the next couple days. Not only will your kids be glad you did, but you will be as well.

CUSTOM NEEDS

We've talked about several needs that your children have, but I've left out some very specific ones that are tailor fit for your children. They may not be needs of my children or your friend's children, but they could be definite needs of your children.

Let me give you an example. My oldest son Ben needs me to listen to him. He has more questions than a Washington Press Corps member, and he needs me to actively listen. Sam, on the other hand, needs me to draw with him.

He loves to draw and asks me on many occasions, "Dad, can you draw with me?" I usually give him the standard dad answer, "Yeah, maybe later," which really means 'never.'

Katherine needs quality time where we lie on her bed and talk about everything.

Isaac needs me to play games with him.

Abe needs me to watch him do things.

Maggie...needs me to hold her.

When I don't meet the specific needs of each of my children, I provoke them to anger.

So what are the specific needs of your children? Each one's are probably different, but their needs are very real.

Take a few minutes and write down each of your children's names on the lines below. Write each one's greatest "need" next to his/her name.

Child #1 _____

Child #2 _____

Child #3 _____

Child #4 _____

Now think about those needs. How can you begin to meet them today? The problem with specific needs is sometimes they seem extreme, and we're tempted to make light of them because they seem silly. I mean doesn't it seem silly that Sam would want his "old" dad to color with him? How many dads color with their children?

But, if I blow it off, I provoke him to anger. Your children (young and old) want something that only you can offer. There are counterfeits out there trying to lure them away from you, and your children will take the bait if they can't get the real thing...the real Father Power.

FATHER POWER TOOLS WE DON'T NEED

I mentioned earlier that whenever I speak to a group of dads, I ask the question, "What do our children need from us?" After speaking to thousands of dads, no one has EVER answered, "A lot of money...a nice car...a father with an important job...great vacations on tropical islands...a healthy retirement account...a nicely manicured lawn...fame...a big house...stock options...a membership at the country club.

Why is it that dads never name those things? It's because they know that none of that stuff matters to children. The only person those things matter to is US. We can say that the reason we work so many hours is so that we can provide these things for our children, but the reality is they don't even need those things. Sadly, we deprive them of the things they do need because we're too busy going after the things they don't need.

Repeat after me.

Cars don't matter—they can be rusty, shiny, cheap, or expensive...but they don't matter.

Houses don't matter.

Furniture doesn't matter.

Big bank accounts don't matter.

European shoes don't matter.

Golf doesn't matter.

Hobbies don't matter.

Big ministries don't matter.

Careers don't matter.

Abs of steel don't matter.

Stuff doesn't matter.

Family matters!!

So the question begs asking, if these things really don't matter, why do we spend most of our time trying to get them?

Let that simmer.

THE ANGER IN PROVOKING TO ANGER

Have you noticed that there are a lot of angry kids in our society? Some children snarl or throw fits and objects;

others say hateful words and curse, and some destroy property, steal, and kill.

Experts and politicians tell us it's because they're victims. But the only truth in that is that they are victims of fathers who withheld from them something that they needed.

Your children may not kill anyone or take a bat to the wall, but that doesn't mean they're not victims as well. There is another facet of provoking to anger...a deceptively quiet side.

Apparently, the Ephesian dads weren't the only ones who needed confrontation. In Paul's letter to the Colossians, we're given additional information as to the extent of Father Power gone awry. Paul gave the same instruction to the Colossian dads, but this time he added a phrase that he hadn't included in the Ephesian's letter.

"Dads, don't provoke your children,
that they may not lose heart" (Colossians 3:21).

To 'lose heart' means to become discouraged and give up. Maybe you've felt that way when you didn't get a promotion you wanted, can't afford a certain car, or feel frustrated with losing weight. After a while, you lose heart, give up, and quit trying. You resolve yourself to the job that you have, the rusty beater you drive, and decide you might as well just give up exercising.

The same thing happens to kids when dads withhold what they really need—they lose heart. They give up and say, "What's the use?" Although I didn't stick around that day to witness the outcome of Mr. Bandanna Guy and his pit bull, I assume that the big dog eventually quit trying to get the stick. Children will do the same if we don't give them what they desperately need. They will quit trying, hoping, and reaching out.

Have you seen the faces of children that this has happened to? Where smiles should be worn, troubled faces are worn instead. They look burdened, unhappy, and withdrawn. The natural desire for hugs and kisses has been replaced by coolness and aloofness. These children grow up with damaged hearts. As adults they might try all kinds of techniques and substitutes to cover up their wounded hearts, but their eyes and faces betray them.

Maybe you have a child that has lost heart. Maybe you have one who used to be all smiles and giggles but now seems sad and sober. Dad, don't write it off as maturity. Could it be that he just hasn't gotten his fill of dad?

Let me share a little bit about my princess Katherine and how I was provoking her to anger. My little girl came out of the womb hugging and caressing. She loved to be held and would suck her thumb and stroke my hair for hours if I let her.

As she grew older, she still loved to sit on my lap or have me lie in bed with her as she held me and giggled about father/daughter things. Along with all that hugging came a lot of girly emotion. She would cry when she got hurt, cry when she felt sad, and cry when she just felt like crying.

At times, it was more than I could stand, and I started scolding her for her emotion and talking harshly when I should have spoken gently and offered comfort. You know what eventually happened? She began to pull away from me. She no longer wanted me sit on her bed with her, and when I pulled her onto my lap, she struggled to free herself.

My little princess was becoming de-princessfied...and I was to blame.

Upon realizing what I had done, I determined to get back my gentle princess so I went on a full-scale hugging and loving attack. I responded gently to her emotions. I told her she was beautiful, lingered by her bed at nighttime, and stroked her hair and talked. And ever since, I have worked extra hard to be the model dad to my little girl.

Guess what? My princess came back, but if I don't keep working at it, I could lose her again.

My fellow dad, that's **father power**.

OK, let's look again at the verse we've been discussing. *"Father's STOP provoking your children to anger"* (Ephesians 6:4a).

Let's translate this into real simple terms.

"Dads, STOP withholding your time, your affection, your listening ear, your fun, your love, and all the other things that your children so desperately want and need from you because it causes them to lose heart and give up."

Why?

Father power.

Now that we've looked at what we're supposed to STOP doing, let's see what we're supposed to BE doing as fathers instead.

DAD 2 DAD (ON YOUR OWN OR IN A GROUP)

1. Who is the main disciplinarian in your house?

   Do you think your wife would like you to take a more active role in disciplining your children?

   Do your children respond better when you or your wife does the discipline?

2. Do you think your children feel unconditionally loved by you?

   If not, what might be one of the conditions they "feel" it's dependent upon?

3. Do you show that you like your kids? Do you smile at them, enjoy being with them, and include them?

4. How would you rank yourself on a fun scale of 1-10? What is the most fun you ever had with your children? How long ago was that?

5. Fill in the blank, "I know my kids would like me to say 'sure' to _____."

6. List one special 'custom' need of each of your children.

7. Would you say that you have any angry children? Could it be that you're not meeting one of his/her needs?

   What might it be and what could you start doing in the next 3 days to meet that need?

Your Prime Directive

"Fathers...instead bring them up in the
training and instruction of the Lord."
Ephesians 6:4

Thankfully, Paul didn't end his instruction with a slam to the head. Instead, he quickly followed it up with the simple instruction:

"...Dads bring your sons and daughters up in the training and instruction of the Lord."

Although the English version doesn't show it, the original text says it more like this..."But YOU, dads, not someone else, feed them in the training and instruction of the Lord..." The emphasis of the instruction is on "YOU".

Paul made it clear that it is the dad's responsibility to bring his children up in the Lord, and to nurture them as though he is literally feeding them the foods that they need

You know you're too busy when...

...the only way your family can talk to you is through email.

to survive and be healthy. Notice he did not say, "Dads, it's your responsibility to make sure <u>someone</u> is training and instructing your children in the Lord." Paul made it crystal clear that the dads are to do the training and the instructing themselves. It is their prime directive.

Apparently, even back then, some dads were handing off the child rearing to the women folk. Besides being too busy, they were duped into thinking that bath times, bedtimes, and bible stories were women's work. Man's job was to kill lions, giants, and sit in the city gates and shoot the breeze with other dads who were neglecting their responsibilities.

Not much has changed in two thousand years. Not only are we dads giving up our teaching to schools and training to churches, but now we're also giving up the best stuff to our wives. We've decided that our job is to bring home the bacon, rest in the evening, and shoot the breeze with other guys who believe the same.

Many women have become the spiritual leaders in their families, the disciplinarians, and the total caregivers, while the dads, sit back, criticize, and occasionally toss in their two bits.

I'm guilty. Every once in a while, I come home to a wife who looks like she's spent a long day wrestling alligators. She's snappy, tired, and sometimes at the end of her rope.

Being the sensitive husband that I am, I sit down and ask her about her day. I listen thoughtfully as she talks about the kids and how frustrated she is because they don't obey, are lazy, and make messes faster than she can keep up.

Then, I quit listening and interrupt her saying, "Well, you need to make them obey. If you let them get away with it once, they'll push the limit every time. What you should do is make them do all the cleaning...maybe you could even make a chart, and give them a mark for every infraction...adding up to a loss of privileges..."

Ooo, I'm on a roll. In fact, I'm surprised when my wife doesn't throw her arms around my neck and thank me for solving her problems. She looks more like she'd like to throw her arms around my neck and strangle me.

The truth is she doesn't need my advice; she needs me to lead the training because it's my responsibility.

It's Your Job

We homeschool our children, but don't be too impressed. Homeschooling is hard, and we struggle our way through it much of the time. But I believe with all my heart, that it is my job to be a homeschooling dad. I also believe it's your job too.

Now don't get me wrong. I didn't say you need to homeschool; I only said you need to be a homeschooling dad. In fact, I know lots of dads who homeschool their children who AREN'T homeschooling dads, and I know dads who don't homeschool their children who ARE homeschooling dads.

My dad was a homeschooling dad, yet my brothers, sister, and I attended a public school. He just believed it was his responsibility to train us for life. He didn't use a blackboard or a textbook, but the lessons he taught me as a child are some of the same ones I've taught my children.

Things like:

• The best lessons are the ones that cost the most.

• If you're not doing anything wrong, it means you're not doing anything.

• Just because he's being mean doesn't mean you have to be mean.

• Sometimes you just have to say, "Enough. It's time to quit."

• Being nice is better than being smart.

• When you're a big boy, you have to make big boy decisions.

• If it's the law, there is no question about if it's right or wrong.

• Always wear your seatbelt, brush your teeth, and wear hard-toed shoes when cutting grass.

We had a set of 1972 World Book Encyclopedias on a shelf in our house when I was growing up and my dad was constantly reading from them. I was home last week and there was a volume sitting right beside his throne. I can remember on many occasions when a topic would come up during dinner, and my dad would say, "Let's see what the encyclopedia says about that."

We'd cringe and plead with him not to get the volume from the shelf, but it was no use. He was up and back at his place flipping through the pages in search of the information that just couldn't wait.

Why did he do that? I believe it's because he took his responsibility of fathering, teaching, and training seriously. He also made choices not to go out with the guys, to be home in the evenings and on the weekends, and to have a career that allowed him to be home with his family.

He was a great dad. He was a homeschooling dad. He still is. Often on the phone, he guides me, encourages me, and cheers me on. In fact, the only reason you are reading this book is because of my dad. When I told him I wanted to be a writer, he said, "You don't want to live your life with any "I wish I would have's," Todd, so, go for it!"

You tell me what son doesn't want to hear those words from his father? Why?

Father power!

TWO ASPECTS OF FATHERING

There are two aspects to your fathering prime directive: 1) training and 2) instruction.

TRAINING

One aspect of our fathering is the training side. It's the hands on, no pain, no gain, get down and get dirty side. It lives in the trenches and is a powerful teacher. It's not just telling your children what they are to do, it's about your example and making them do it...and then dolling out consequences when they don't.

It's the "Coach Burrow's principle." He was my football coach in high school. He stood about five and a half feet tall, had fiery red hair, and was a master of training young athletes.

His coaching model was pretty simple. Work them hard, yell a lot, and make their mistakes hurt so they won't make them again. I was an offensive end so my job was to catch anything the quarterback threw my way. One drill Mr. Burrows liked was where all the "catchers" stood in a line about ten yards opposite him, and as we ran toward him, he rifled a football at our chests.

For anyone who hasn't ever tried it, it's tough and kind of scary running towards a bullet in the gut. Sometimes I caught it, sometimes I didn't. When I didn't, he'd yell, "Give me a lap, Wilson."

I knew the routine. It was a stair lap around the gym, or worse, around the practice field. When I returned, I got back in line, and ran towards him again, more determined than ever to catch that ball.

Now, I'm certainly not telling you to act like my high school football coach in all ways. His training methods didn't make me like him a whole bunch, but it did teach me to catch the football...but not good enough to play in the NFL.

But there are things you can learn from his example and apply in training your children.

SET A LEVEL OF EXPECTATION

Dad, it's up to you to set the level of expectation for your children. Yes, you should talk it over with your wife, seek godly instruction and pray about it, but ultimately, you are responsible for the level you set for your children.

If you want them to be kind to each other, then tell them what's expected of them and make sure you model kindness. If you want them to talk respectfully to you, then make it clear that's what you expect and make sure you talk respectfully to your wife and others. If you need to write it somewhere in your house for all to see, then go ahead.

Please pick your expectations carefully. You will exasperate your children if you place too many expectations on them. Start with a few. Call a family meeting after dinner and tell the kids in training what will be expected of them and what the outcome will be if they fail to meet those expectations.

If you do that, you will have accomplished two things: your wife will love you for taking the lead, and you will have drawn a visible line that the children can see and deal with.

FOLLOW THROUGH

I'm tempted to use the phrase "be consistent", but I hate that phrase. It's not that it's bad or unbiblical; it's just that I have such a problem being consistent, and I know a lot of other dads and moms who do as well.

Instead, I'll just say, "Follow through with your game plan." If you have required that your kids be kind to one another, and you find them fighting like cats and dogs, you must step in and handle it.

With Coach Burrows, it was a lap. I knew it; he knew it; we all knew it. In fact, even before the ball dropped to the ground, I was already off to take my lap. There was no argument and no excuses; I just did it.

That's consistent. That's follow through. Every time. No exceptions. If a child fails to meet the standard set by you, there are consequences to pay.

CONSEQUENCES

The consequences of not rising to the level of expectation have to sting. My football consequence was a lap. The consequence you set will be something else. Now don't confuse the word consequence with punishment. We do not punish our children when they don't do what was expected of them. We train them, and we discipline them, but we don't get "even with them" because they let us down.

Instead, the consequence must sting because we love them, and we want to train them in right behavior. The key words are sting and love.

Pain is a great teacher. You learned early that if you touch something hot, it burns so you stay away from it. If the pain were removed there would be little to keep you from placing your hand right on a stove burner.

The key is to choose the most effective pain or the best teacher. So, if you've set the expectation that your children will be kind to each other, and you find them being unkind, you must do something that will train them to be kind.

One consequence might be the loss of a privilege. If they're watching a video and fight over who controls the remote, the consequence might be not getting to watch the video.

Don't allow them to challenge you, and don't back down when they give you all their "good" excuses. Tell them to take a lap and do it.

Dad, if you follow through with a painful discipline, they will soon learn not to break the expectation set by you.

Follow-Up

The final aspect of training involves talking and affection. Coach Burrows never did this part of training. He never once pulled me on his lap to tell me how much he loved me and what he expected of me (not that I fault him...it may have been a little weird coming from my football coach.)

You must not skip this last and most important part of training and discipline. It's where you talk with your child about what happened, why it happened, what God says about it, and how it affects others.

You remind your children how much you love them and how proud you are of them. Sometimes forgiveness needs to be asked and/or given, and then you pray.

Believe me Dad, this kind of training instructs and teaches lessons for life. As I mentioned earlier, it's one of the things that children need from their dad. They need you to spank them, to discipline them, to give them boundaries, to hold them, and to pray with them.

That's your job. Don't pawn it off on your wife or blame society. Your children need you to discipline them in the Lord and you can do it. You 'da dad!

Children who are not disciplined (trained) are provoked to anger and lose heart.

You know why?

Father Power.

INSTRUCTION

The other side of the fathering coin is instruction. By instruction, I don't mean a super-dad who gets up early with his children and spends an hour studying theological doctrines from scripture or some kind of Ward Cleaver dad who always has a scripted answer for every circumstance.

The instruction side of fathering is simply teaching your children about life, God, and his/her place in His plan. It isn't about a curriculum; it's about spending time together and passing along what you believe.

Let's hold onto this thought until we talk more about it in chapter 6. For now, answer and discuss the Dad 2 Dad questions.

DAD 2 DAD (ON YOUR OWN OR IN A GROUP)

1. Have you established a clear set of expectations for your children?

2. List a few "issues" that each of your children is facing and then list an appropriate "chastisement for each offense next to it.
   (Ex. My child argues when I ask him to turn off the video he is watching or the game he is playing. Consequence: he will not be allowed to watch or play the next scheduled time.)

3. Of the 4 parts of discipline, which is most difficult for you...and why?

   • Expectation

   • Follow through

   • Consequences

   • Follow-up

4. What 5 character traits would you most like to see in your children?

5. What practical steps can you do to help them acquire these?

6. Are you willing to change your schedule if necessary to accomplish this?

7. If not, what's holding you back from doing that?

8. What might your children turn out like if you don't teach them what they need to be taught?

9. What do you need to do today to make changes and begin the process?

The Heart of a Super Dad

The Original "Promise Keepers"

Did you know that Paul wasn't the first person to give fathers advice? Moses gave much of the same instruction 3000 years before Paul wrote to the dads in Ephesus. So let's go back to the time of Moses and imagine what the first "Promise Keepers" rally in recorded in history was like.

Picture a sea of people praising God and sharing how He had delivered them from bondage. Suddenly a hush came over the crowd and a small man stepped to the impromptu podium. His face radiated brilliance, and in his arms he held two stone tablets. There was no sound system, but his voice rose in a commanding tone.

Everyone was quiet as he recited the commandments of God. It took awhile, but he made his way to the end of the list.

Then he continued, and what he said next is known to-day among the Jews as the 'Shema.' The words that were uttered on that mountainside that day continue to begin the service of most Jewish synagogues today.

"Shema Israel! (Hear, O Israel) the Lord our God, the Lord is One. Love the Lord your God with all your heart and with all your soul and with all your strength. These commandments that I give to you today are to be upon your hearts. Teach them diligently to your children..."

I call this the first "Promise Keepers" rally because Moses was talking to dads, and everyone knew that dads were the ones responsible to train their children.

"...Teach them diligently to your children. Talk about them when you sit at home and when you walk along the road, when you lie down and when you get up. Tie them as symbols on your hands and bind them on your foreheads. Write them on the door frames of your house and on your gates...be careful that you do not forget the Lord who brought you out of Egypt, out of the land of slavery" (Deuteronomy 6:4-12).

I imagine there was a deafening roar, applause, and whoops and hollers in response to the command. Fathers were pumped up and convicted concerning their role and responsibility for future generations of Yahweh followers. They knew they had The Power!

"Father Power...Father Power...Father Power," they might have chanted with clenched fists lifted into the air. Could fathering really be that simple, that important, and that profound?

Yes!

That's what the latter part of the Ephesian passage is all about. It was true for the fathers of 3000 BC, the fathers in Ephesus, and it is still true for you today.

FATHER POWER BEGINS IN THE HEART

In Moses' instruction he shared with them (and you) the secret of successfully wielding the father power that has been entrusted to you. It's the same instruction one dad received when he asked, "What makes a good dad?"

The answer? Be prepared; it has the potential to rock your world.

Moses began his instruction addressing the heart of the father. That's where Father Power begins.

"Love God with all YOUR heart and with all YOUR soul and with all YOUR strength. These commandments that I give to YOU today are to be upon YOUR hearts" *(Deuteronomy 6:5).*

He knew fathers couldn't lead, train, or instruct their children until they have dealt with their own hearts. Dads can't help shape their children beyond where they are themselves.

Telling children, "Don't do as I do, do as I say," doesn't work. Children grow up doing as their parents do, going where they go, saying what they say, and being what they are. Why?

Father Power.

That's the hardest part about fathering, isn't it? I'd much rather tell my children what to do than to lead them by example. If I tell them to trust God for all the little things and then fall apart when some unplanned circumstance comes my way, guess what they learn?

They learn from me that God can't be trusted.

If I tell the kids to be kind to one another and then I speak to my wife harshly, they learn to be mean, yell, and demand their own way.

If I tell them to obey the law, and then they see my speedometer needle 15 miles beyond the speed limit, they learn to pick and choose which laws to obey.

I wish Moses had said, "Now all this stuff I've just talked about...make sure those kids of yours do it!" But he didn't. He pointed his stony finger in their chest and said, "Dad, it starts with you. Love God with all you have and let these commandments be in your innermost being. Make them your own."

Moses didn't intend love for God to be measured by the "religious exercises" they did, but he was reminding a bunch of dads to go to God for life, wisdom, security, and everything else.

THESE COMMANDMENTS

Besides loving God with all their hearts, Moses wanted the dads to make God's commandments their own. Let me list the "big 10" for you here:

1. You shall have no other Gods before me.
2. You shall not have or worship idols.
3. You shall not use God's name in vain.
4. Remember the Sabbath and keep it holy.
5. Honor your father and mother.
6. You shall not murder.

7. You shall not commit adultery.

8. You shall not steal.

9. You shall not lie.

10. You shall not covet what others have.

These commandments were to be in their hearts, and they are to be in yours as well. It's not just a list to be posted on a courthouse lawn somewhere in rural America. It's God's truth boiled down into one long paragraph (a good memorization project).

When God said, "You shall have no other God before Me," he meant that you're not to put anything or anyone else in God's place. That means your job must not become your god, your hobbies must not become your god, and your bank account must not become your god. God is to be number one in your life.

How do you know if something else has taken God's place? You look at your calendar, your checkbook, and ask your wife. Those things will tell you where you spend your time, your money, and your attentions.

Has something taken God's place? I know it doesn't take much contemplation before I come up with half a dozen "gods" that have pushed Him aside.

So what do you do to put God back in his rightful place? You do what they did in the Old Testament when an idle or false god had replaced God; you tear it down, burn it up, grind it up, and obliterate it.

Sound drastic? Yes! But that's what it means to have these commands upon your heart.

We've covered one; there are still nine more to go! Here's the list again. I left a little space after each one in which to jot a few notes. Be honest. Are these commands yours? Do you need to rethink how you're living in light of commandments #5...#7...#10?

1. You shall have no other God's before me.

    (Has anything become more important to me than God? If yes, list it.)

2. You shall not have or worship idols.

    (Do I have any possessions, hobbies, or habits that have become idols (or others might call idols)? List them.)

3. You shall not use God's name in vain.

    (Am I carelessly using God's name in vain? What words do I need to cut out?)

4. Remember the Sabbath and keep it holy.

    (Am I working away my day of rest?)

5. Honor your father and mother.

    (How am I treating my parents?)

6. You shall not murder.

   (Have I killed people with my words or actions? Matthew 5:21-26)

7. You shall not commit adultery.

   (Are all my relationships and thoughts pure? Matthew 5:27-28)

8. You shall not steal.

   (Have I been stealing in little things?)

9. You shall not lie.

   (Am I totally honest at work, home, church?)

10. You shall not covet what others have.

    (Have I been envious of what others have?)

PASS IT ON

   "...Teach them diligently to your children" *(Deuteronomy 6:7).*

   The ultimate reason God wants you to have these commands in your heart is so that you can pass them on to your children so that they can pass them on to their children and so impact the world.

But it's not enough for you to go to church and know the Bible. You must live it and teach it to your children. Otherwise, they might grow up and turn their backs on God and the church.

Moses used a peculiar word in his instruction, one that is used nowhere else in the entire Bible. It's the word "to sharpen."

When he said, "Impress them upon your children," he was really saying, "Sharpen your children." The word was chosen carefully, and it paints a vivid picture of what is involved in fathering.

SHARPENING 101

I like tools, and I've done a little sharpening in my life. I've noticed that my blades become dull after awhile, especially chisels. They cut through wood like butter when they're new, but after some time, they begin to tear the wood instead of cut the wood. Dull blades make the work tougher and the outcome ugly.

To remedy the dull, smooth blade, I walk over to my ancient-looking bench grinder and slam the dull chisel against the wheel sending a shower of sparks onto my legs. A minute later, I examine the chisel's freshly ground edge and get back to work.

If you know anything about woodworking, then the way I sharpen blades should make you cringe. I know it's the wrong way, but I just don't have the patience to do it the right way.

The right method involves using different sharpening stones, various speeds, and polishing. It is way more involved than my bench grinder method. I once saw a book on sharpening in a wood worker's catalogue that was 366 pages long. It talked about different Japanese sharpening stones...natural verses synthetic...angles and strokes.

How in the world can a book about sharpening have 366 pages? I could have written the book in less than 366 WORDS. But as I watch woodworking shows and observe real craftsmen, I see that their tools work better than mine, cut better than mine, and last longer than mine.

Real craftsman even sharpen the blade when they take it out of the package for the first time feeling that the factory edge isn't good enough.

Sharpening a blade is a picture of the fathering process. You can't use my old bench grinder method. You can't slam into them and make a lot of sparks, by taking them to church, or getting them in a good school and expect that to do the job. It's just not good enough.

Training children is more like the rhythmic pattern of using a Japanese sharpening stone, and then a smaller grit stone, and then a smaller grit stone, and then polishing it to a mirror finish. It's teaching them to trust and love God and His word a little at a time, until it's all the time.

The only problem with the 366-page parenting (sharpening) method is that it takes so much time and effort. My bench grinder method is the equivalent of a book entitled, "The One Minute Father."

Actually "The One Minute Father" would be a bestseller. It's what men want: something that tells them how to have a great family with less than one minute of their involvement a day."

Bench grinder fathering gets bench grinder results. To have children that love God, honor parents, obey God's word, live productive godly lives, and turn out to be the kind of children we desire, we have to do the 366-page kind of sharpening fathering.

Fortunately, Moses explained how to do just that...in less than 366 pages. Being a father himself, he reduced the instruction manual down to 50 words, and by the time we're finished, I will have whittled it down to **two words**.

DAD 2 DAD (ON YOUR OWN OR IN A GROUP)

1. Since all this Father Power begins with you, how are you doing regarding the list on pages 90-91?

2. Is it possible that some of the things your children struggle with are things they learned from you? List these things.

3. Pick one of these struggles and take one step towards correcting it.
    (Ex. If you have trouble being affectionate with your family, then plan to touch each of your children once each day and hug your wife before you leave for work.)

4. Now, list one way you can "sharpen" your children in this area as well.

BE THERE

"Talk about them when you sit at home and when you walk along the road, when you lie down and when you get up. Tie them as symbols on your hands and bind them on your foreheads. Write them on the door frames of your house and on your gates...be careful that you do not forget the Lord who brought you out of Egypt, out of the land of slavery." (Deuteronomy 6:4-12)

THE BAT CAVE OF FATHERING

This chapter brings us to the bowels of what it means to be a dad and how to wield this great power with which we've been entrusted. After winding our way through the importance of being a father, and the results of provoking our children, we are now ready to discover the bat cave of fathering.

It's interesting that Moses really didn't talk about HOW to instruct our children other than to say, "sharpen them."

Instead, he focused on the 'when' and 'where' that instruction should take place, because if you take care of the when and where, the rest will take care of itself.

These were the instructions of Moses:

Talk about God's commandments...

...at home

...on the road

...at bedtime

...at breakfast time

AT HOME

In a nutshell, Moses said, "OK Dads, you need to love God and follow His word, and then with the same intensity as following a 366-page sharpening guide, you need to teach your children to do the same. So...talk about all these things when you're sitting at home."

Now I know what you're thinking: Moses is talking about family devotions—the bane of dads everywhere. I think we've been made to believe that's what Moses was talking about—by women. But it's not. He's not talking about a classroom in your home where you have to sit down and wade through Biblical instruction either.

Moses was talking to dads, not college professors. Besides that kind of instruction rarely works with children. I know because I've tried. I used to think godly families had family devotions where everyone sat and listened for hours as the dad read through long passages of begets and pages of doctrine. The children would then discuss it, apply it to their lives, and run out the door to win the world for Christ...or at least clean their rooms without being told.

Yeah, right. Our family devotions look more like a cross between championship wrestling and Fear Factor. I spend more time disciplining than I do instructing, and most of the time, I feel like chucking the whole thing out the window...including them.

Actually, children learn best when it's part of life. I think Moses knew that, which is why that lies at the heart of his instructions to dads.

He said, "Just talk to your kids when you're at home." Sound simple? It is. It's not about easels or lesson plans. It doesn't involve timelines or complex doctrines. It just involves dads talking to children about God in the midst of life.

It's **Father Power** in action.

Here's what it looks like. It's a dad leading his family to God and asking him to provide for their needs when finances get tight. It's a dad modeling trust for his children as they wait for God to answer.

It's dads sitting around the dinner table and talking to the kids about school, the neighborhood, and news on TV. It's a dad asking, "So what do you think the president should do?" Or, "What do you think it would feel like to have all of your family killed in a mud slide?"

It's children coming to fathers when they have been hurt or when they need to confess. It's dads disciplining children for failing to rise to the standard.

It's dads praying and playing without much distinction between the two. It's dads walking beside their children through life...pointing out God.

Doesn't that sound better than sitting down with a Bible curriculum and struggling through a story and application? You tell me, which is more effective in training your children?

Father power.

The only drawback is the time involved. It's much quicker to do the Bible study/ devotion method for a few minutes a day and you're done (think bench grinder). The method Moses was advocating takes 24/7. All day, every day. It will wear you out and spit you out a tired, rumpled mess.

But that's fathering and it's worth it.

Note: If you're interested in more information regarding family devotions, I've included some helps in the appendix at the back of the book.

IN THE CAR

In addition to training children at home, Moses added, "...train them when you're riding in the car." Actually he said, "When you're walking along the road," but not many dads walk along the road with their kids anymore. What he's trying to convey is that some of the best training times take place when a father and child are traveling from point A to point B.

Great things happen when you're in the car alone with one of your children.

Unfortunately though, sometimes we dads look at driving time as peace and quiet time. So when we have to run to the hardware store, we sneak out the door and jump in the car before anyone knows we're missing.

Actually, since I work out of the home, I love short rides alone. That was until my talk with Bob.

One dreary day in Duluth, MN, my friend Bob and his family were sitting in our RV as the cold rain fell outside. I'm not sure what we were talking about but out of his mouth came, "Dads should never go anywhere without taking along a child for the ride."

I agreed. It is a good way to avoid temptations. That's not what he meant.

"I mean you should never go anywhere without taking along a kid," he said emphatically. "Never ever. Even if you're just going to the hardware store, you need to take along a kid. Because great things happen in the car."

I was thinking about that just the other day when I had to make the two-minute trip to the post office. My son asked to go along, but I said, "Not this time...it will just take a minute." Bob's instruction rang in my head, but I ignored it, all the while regretting my mistake.

Some of my best fatherly memories are car rides with one of my kids, whether it's a deep conversation with Ben, giggles with Sam, or tender hand holding with my little princess. Bob is right—great things happen in the car.

The best thing is that you don't have to pass out notes or an outline of topics of discussion. In fact, you probably won't have to saying anything at first. Usually, your child will start the conversation. Now if you have older kids and haven't fostered this car time, you may have to initiate the talk time. Ask what their favorite memory of summer is or what they'd like to do for their birthday...or anything else 'safe.' Don't feel like you have to guide it to some spiritual conversation...because they are all spiritual conversations.

You can spend the entire car ride talking about squirrels, and you will have taught your child that you care about what's important to him, because he is important to you...and God feels the same way.

Talk about a lot of bang for your buck! Moses knew what he was talking about.

BEDTIME

The next 'when' that Moses named is bedtime. Now, don't read into the instruction or assume that means bedtime devotions. Although bedtime might include devotions, it doesn't have to, and I'm positive that Moses didn't intend bedtime devotions.

How could he have? Writing had just been invented so there weren't even copies of the Bible available yet. But somehow we've gotten it into our heads that we have to read a chapter of the Bible every night before bed, pray for the 10/40 window, and give an alter call.

I had one well-meaning mother come up to me after she found out I talk to dads, and tell me, "You need to tell those men to have family devotions. They need to lead their family to Christ and teach them the Bible and the doctrines of the faith."

I looked at her like—who do you think men are...WOMEN?

I said, "Hey, I'm just trying to get dads to be involved in bedtime."

That's what Moses was talking about. That's what I'm asking you to do. Be involved in bedtime. For some reason, most dads have passed on this responsibility to their wives.

Often dads give half-hearted kisses to children and pat them off to bed as they sit in their recliners watching TV or type away on their computer while mom does the hard work.

That's not the way it is supposed to be. Just like car time, bedtime is a magical time. The lights are dim, the children wind down, and hearts are opened. They are primed and ready to talk.

If you're like this big clod of a dad, you blow it. I put kids to bed like I'm being timed for the Olympic bedtime trials.

"Brush your teeth...Get in bed...Ike where are you?...Katherine this room is a pit...Come on boys, let's get moving."

I zip through prayers, threaten a couple of the younger ones, and half-heartedly read a chapter or two out of a book that seems to be forever long. Man, I forget about father power!

But when I slow down and curl up in bed with a child, something special happens. I can usually tell when it's about to happen because things get real quiet and they hold me extra tight.

"Dad," my daughter Katherine might say softly, "The girls at church were talking about such and such, and I felt bad for Christi." At that moment, she's just invited me into the private world of her heart.

I have to be careful when her heart opens. I must tread softly and ask more questions than I answer. I stroke her forehead and kiss her cheek. I tell her how proud I am of her and how well she responded.

I don't correct. I encourage. We pray and she clings to me when I try to leave. She wants more...Oh, and I should give her more, BUT I'm busy. Always busy.

I once interviewed a dad who lost his entire family in a flash flood. He was a great dad. He talked about how he would spend an hour every night putting the kids down. He would lie in their beds and ask about their day, what they liked most, and what they didn't. He would sing with them and pray with them and for them.

He was a great dad, and now they're all gone.

But his children are in heaven because he spent time with them at bedtime, because it's then that children often say, "Dad, I'm afraid to die."

That's when dads pass on the good news to their children that Jesus loves them and died so they don't have to.

But this training can't happen if you pass it onto your wife or are too busy to be involved.

Let me give you the 5 minute challenge, dad. Tonight, determine in your heart to spend 5 whole minutes with each child at bedtime. Crawl into their beds or kneel beside them and ask them about their day. Let them talk, while you stroke their side or hold their hand. It doesn't matter if they're 2 years old or 18 years old. Every child loves that time with dad. Why?

Father power!

Vowing to eat breakfast with his family, Steve
found it easier than he anticipated.

Breakfast Time

I'm not sure what the statistics are, but I would just about bet that most men don't eat breakfast with their families. I understand the reason for those numbers. The early morning hours are prime hours to get paperwork accomplished before the phone starts ringing. The office is quiet and two hours before 8 a.m. is the equivalent of 5 prime-time working hours. Plus, there just aren't enough working hours to get it all done otherwise.

Every morning, millions of dads tiptoe down hallways hoping to let sleeping kids lie. And every morning, millions of children wake up to homes where dad has already jumped ship.

Mornings around the breakfast table serve as great training times. Children are moving slow (or at least slower) and are able to absorb interactions better.

It's a time where dads can talk about the coming day and its set of circumstances. Prayer takes place for tests, ball games, and their witness in the world. In fact, if there were ever an easier time for devotions, breakfast time would be it.

Think baby steps. You don't have to teach them everything every morning. Just a little here and a little there. In fact, you don't always have to teach, sometimes you might just pray or talk about an area that needs special attention that day.

You might give coaching on an expected behavior or memorize a Bible verse. Manage your expectations and set the bar low. Remember this is 366-page sharpening fathering not bench grinder fathering.

Dad, even if you do nothing except take up space at the breakfast table, you are still training and teaching your children volumes. You teach them that family is more important than work, that work must have limits, and that dad is committed to his family.

That's **Father Power** at it's best!

So in a nutshell, *"Bringing them up in the training and instruction of the Lord" (Ephesians 6:4)* is the same as *"Sharpen them at home, in the car, at bedtime and at the breakfast table" (Deuteronomy 6:7)*.

But remember:

You can't sharpen them at home, if you're not home.

You can't sharpen them in the car, if you're not there for car rides.

You can't sharpen them at bedtime, if you're not there for bedtime.

You can't sharpen them at the breakfast table, if your seat is empty.

You can't train and instruct your children in the Lord if you are not there to train and instruct, AND

You provoke your children to anger, and they lose heart because you are not there.

Read that again.

So the secret of **Father Power** boiled down into two words is:

BE THERE!

That, my fellow father, is the secret to being a good dad. It's not about never yelling at your kids, always being consistent, or being a spiritual giant, because we all fall short in these areas. A good dad is one who is there for his children. He is there at dinnertime, bath time, playtime, good time, bad time, bedtime, and morning time. He goes to ball games and plays ball. He builds tree houses and dollhouses. He's there to talk about Legos and deep spiritual matters. **He's there**.

Dads have many excuses as to why they can't be there however. A dad can argue that his job demands the time, that he's just trying to be a good testimony, or that it is only for a season, but he cannot avoid the responsibility and instructions given my Moses, Paul, and God. The truth is, he's letting his children down and will one day regret it.

Why?

FATHER POWER!!!!!!

So let me ask you this question, Dad.

Are you there?

Are you there when the kids get up? Are you there at dinnertime? Are you there at bedtime? Do you have the time to run errands with your children? Are you there to train and instruct? OR,

Are you too busy making a living that you've forgotten to make a life? Are you so busy with what you think is important that you've neglected what's really important? Are you on the road several days a week? Do you work well past the kids' bedtimes? Do you play catch up on the weekends by immersing yourself in your projects? Are you just so busy pursuing your career that you've forgotten your prime directive?

Dad, although I'd like to say that you could be a good dad while working like a dog, spending days away on business, and realizing every dream you've ever had, the truth is you can't. You can't delegate your responsibilities to your wife, the school, or the church. You can't even make up for lost time on the weekends because...it's lost. Your children don't need excuses, THEY NEED YOU!!!

How much of you?

ALL OF YOU!

Father Power.

DAD 2 DAD (ON YOUR OWN OR IN A GROUP)

1. How do you 'feel' about the amount of time you spend at home?

   Are you there "enough?"

   Does your family feel like you're there "enough?"

2. What is the strongest pull away from home?

   What would it take to break the pull?

3. What do you think about taking a kid with you wherever you go?

4. Is it easier for you to be "there" at bedtime or breakfast time?

   Which is more important?

   How would you have to rearrange your schedule to be there at those times?

WHERE DID ALL THE DADS GO?

A mom once told me that she and her young children were running an errand in town when they passed by her husband's office. The husband had been gone a lot lately because when the mother and her clan passed the large facility where he worked, the little boy pointed and said, "Look Mommy, that's where daddy lives."

Sadly, I hear too many similar stories. I hear stories of children who cry because their daddy isn't coming home for dinner and stories of children who fall asleep on the couch hoping to awake when their dad comes home from work.

Children are not the only members of the family who suffer. There are also tired, worn out, frustrated wives who desperately need their husbands at home. They do their best to be both mother and father, but God didn't create the family to work that way.

But that's not the worst of it. The worst part is that both children and wives end up moving on with their lives because they've lost heart.

While, shivering outside in the cold, Mark began to realize he spends too much time on the road.

Children have gone from crying to accepting. They no longer set the place at the table for dad or wait up for him to get home. They know that he'll be too tired or too busy on the weekend to do much with them.

Maybe that little boy was on to something. The work place has gone from the place where daddy works to the place where daddy lives.

What happened?

I can't help but ask the question: when did we dads get so dumb? To put it more kindly, when did we start trading diamonds for stones? Was it all of a sudden or was there a gradual shift?

Even yesterday, I heard a report on the radio that suggests that over 40% of all workers put in over 50 hours a week. That means there are a bunch of dads who are putting in a lot of hours.

Generally speaking, dads work too much. They think they're maximizing their earning potential but they're actually squandering their father potential.

DAD THE BREAD WINNER

Has it always been this way? I don't think so...something has changed. It used to be that men considered themselves the family breadwinners. A couple of hundred years ago, men spent their days providing the basic essentials for their families.

There was a house to make out of dirt, dung, or trees. There was food that had to be planted, harvested, or killed. If a dad sloughed off the job, his family either froze to death or starved. It wasn't real complicated, but it was easy to stay focused.

Even then, dads often did the building, farming, and hunting, with their children (old and young) helping alongside. Dads were also responsible to educate and train their children so that they would grow up and be able to do the same for their families. And remember the "truth transmission" that we talked about earlier? Men knew it was their responsibility to train their youngin's in the scripture and spiritual matters because there was no one else to do it.

There was no midweek kids' program down at the church or a CD of Bible stories available at the local Christian bookstore. It was either them or nothing.

But time passed and society became more "sophisticated," and a shift took place from independent families building, killing, and training together to families that moved into the cities to get real jobs.

Now, dads didn't have to build, kill, and train. Instead, they went to work and earned a wage. They bought their shelter, their food, and even sent their kids to a place where someone else would teach them.

Most of the jobs at that time involved physical labor or monotonous tasks. Dad didn't care though; it provided for his family, and the work was steady.

And when dad left his job each day, he left his job. He couldn't catch up on voice mail, email, or crank out a report on his laptop. There were no golf clubs, bowling leagues, or bass tournaments to take up his weekends, and Sunday was still a day when the nation came to a stop and rested...as a family.

DAD THE LUXURY PROVIDER

More time passed as well as a couple of world wars. Technology allowed for luxuries like shiny new cars, modular housing, and plenty of convenient gadgets like blenders, garage door openers, and televisions.

Dad moved from "bread winner" to "convenience provider." After all, he had to keep up with the Jones's, and a good paying job was the ticket to get and keep those things. In fact, if a dad could put in a little overtime he could upgrade those things from time to time and take a vacation to the newly opened Disneyland in California.

So men started working more, so much so, that on the weekends they needed some time to themselves to unwind. Enter the golf clubs, tennis clubs, and stopping off for a drink with the boys.

Television was the thing that brought the family together though. Most evenings, the entire family would gather around the big snowy picture tube to watch Gleason, Uncle Milte, and those boys from Texico.

Although television did have its drawbacks, parents soon discovered that if they sat their kids in front of the TV, then just like magic, they were quiet for hours. TV producers realized that they could grow an audience if they provided shows that would teach and entertain their viewers.

Out of the depths of creativity, rose Captain Kangaroo, Mister Rogers, Bozo the Clown, Kermit the Frog, and hundreds of other local celebrities. It worked. Kids learned all kinds of stuff, from the alphabet to how to get along with others.

It was a great teaching tool...and that meant that dad didn't have to do as much of it anymore. So he didn't. He didn't have to get up with the kids anymore on Saturday morning either. Now all he had to say were the magic words, "Go watch cartoons."

In fact, dad had to do very little of the training anymore. The kids had good schools, good churches, and good television shows. All was well in the dad-world. There were a few struggles in the 60's and 70's, but overall, prosperity was booming and dads were leading the charge.

DAD THE LADDER CLIMBER

Progress was moving along at a pretty good clip until the advent of the computer (this is not an anti-technology chapter). Up until that time, men worked hard to provide the finer things of life, but with the advent of the personal computer, things accelerated to warp speed.

We also saw the transition from bread winner/luxury provider to ladder climber. The stakes were raised to a dangerous level. The carrot in front of the horse got real BIG.

Men went off to college to get a degree...to be something. Most weren't satisfied with being a "worker;" instead they wanted a CAREER, a ministry, or a dream.

All of a sudden, it was as if nitroglycerin had been added to the fire. Now, men worked long hours, went in early, and got home late in order to climb the corporate ladder. If they put in the time, did the work, and could prove to the powers-that-be that they were doing a good job, they would get the coveted "promotion."

This meant they would be placed into a more demanding job where they could work more hours so they could get...another promotion. Which meant...you're way a head of me. The plan was for this to continue until finally you couldn't go any higher. But it wouldn't have mattered because you would have arrived!!!

Of course there would have to be some sacrifices along the way...the family would have to be sacrificed in order for the dad to get to the top...but they would thank him for it one day and understand all the sacrifices he made for them.

All that ladder climbing meant there was little or no time for teaching or training, and in order to make up for his absence, the father put his kids into the best Christian schools, and sent them to the best youth programs and summer camps. After all, a busy kid is a happy kid.

A Change in Game Plan

Another change in the game of life took place. Now, life had to be categorized into to two groups: important stuff and non-important stuff. For example: a son's basketball game might be categorized as important stuff so dad would plan to be there...or at least meet the rest of the family there on his way home from work.

Dance recitals, graduations, and family vacations...all-important—be there. But bedtime, dinnertime, and breakfast...uh...uh...uh...that's non-important so that could be skipped, with the promise of being there for the important stuff.

The problem with this system is that sometimes it's hard to determine what important stuff is. What seems important to a wife might not seem important to a busy, ladder-climbing dad.

That can cause some friction...so Dad promises to change and be there for the "unimportant things," but when a project comes up at work or a deadline must be reached, he determines that the stuff his wife thinks is important isn't really that important because he will have to miss just this once.

That's where we are today, Dad, but the important stuff/non-important stuff model doesn't work. It fails to take into account that it's ALL important.

Bedtime is just as important as a ball game, which is just as important as buying an ice cream cone from the ice cream truck, which is just as important as having a wrestling match on the living room floor, which is just as important as sitting around the breakfast table before school.

It's all important!

Why?

Father power.

WHERE DID DADDY GO?

So the question arises: where did all the dads go? What happened to the dad whose number one priority was his family, who lived his life to provide for them, teach them, and train them for the future? What happened to the dad who felt a deep responsibility to pass along God's truth to his children so that they might do the same for their children?

The simple answer is that he got too busy. It doesn't help that experts, pastors, and authors applaud extreme work ethics and continually spout off such tripe that men get their worth from their jobs.

It hasn't always been that way...and even if it has, it doesn't make it right. A dad's value should come from the family that he raises and the wife that he loves, not from the ladder he climbs. Don't believe me? Go ask an old guy—he'll tell you.

The world needs more dads who give their children what they need to live and love fully, dads who take fathering seriously and are willing to make sacrifices to maximize their Father Power. This kind of dad isn't perfect or some kind of spiritual superman...he just shows up everyday for his most important job.

BE HONEST

Dad, let me ask you to do something potentially painful. I've included a chart for you to fill out. I know, I hate charts too, but take a few minutes and fill in the blanks. Be as honest as you can.

How many hours did you give to your job last week? Include travel time, work-at-home time, lunches, dinners...everything.

Monday	_____
Tuesday	_____
Wednesday	_____
Thursday	_____
Friday	_____
Saturday	_____
Sunday	_____
Total	_____

Out of 7 dinners, how many did you sit down and eat with your family? _____

Out of 7 breakfasts, how many did you sit down and eat with your family? _____

Were you there for at least 5 bedtimes this week?

_____

How many hours did you participate in a hobby or task without your family? _____

Were you able to have lunch with your family on Saturday or Sunday? _____

During the week, did you promise your wife or children something but did not follow through?

_____

Does your wife think you work too much?

_____

Do your children think you work too much?

_____

Have you ever asked them? _____

Are you afraid of their answer? _____

THE VOICE OF GOD

An age-old question is: how many hours are too many hours a week to work? Actually, people who say that there is no magic number are the ones who work too much.

Usually, they say that question can't be answered, but they're wrong. I can't say how many hours are too many, but your wife and children can.

Has your wife asked you to be home more often? Does she seem to nag you about the time you spend on your hobbies or at the office? Have your kids ever asked, "Are you going to be home tonight, tomorrow, or this week?" Dad, you're foolish not to listen to their voices, because God often speaks to us through them.

If your wife has said you work too much, then chances are that you work too much! If your kids think you work too much, chances are you do.

I'm not talking about the occasional week where you put in extra hours, but if that is the norm, then you're stealing hours from your family, you're missing out on God's best, and you're provoking your children to anger.

In fact, you're not doing the task you were commanded and created to do because you're not there.

Let me pause a minute here, because I'm feeling like one of those preachers on TV who gets all sweaty and rants and raves all over the platform thumping the podium like he's driving nails with his fist.

I don't want to come across that way. I know the pressures to succeed are great today. I know you want to provide for your family and do the best job you can. You have dreams and ambitions. I know that. I know you sometimes feel trapped by your family and that there's no easy way out.

I know that, and I feel your frustration and "stuckness.'

But what motivates me to write this book is that I know how the story ends. I've heard men say that their greatest fear is that they're blowing it in the dad department. They know what's most important, but they continue doing what they're doing, hoping that the inevitable will never come.

The truth is: we all end up pursuing what's unimportant from time to time. But here's the good news: it is never too late to start focusing on what's most important, but sometimes you have to make up for lost time.

The choices are clear and must be acted upon. That's what it is all about. It's about making choices. Choosing the important over things that seem important.

It's simple but not easy.

CHOICES

Dad, you've done the math. You've heard about the amazing power that you wield. Your choices today affect your children's future, their marriages, their families, and their theology. Why?

Yep. I've pounded it into the ground...so I'm not even going to say it.

Maybe you've found yourself standing at the end of a dusty road in the middle of a cowboy movie town with two six-shooters strapped to your waist staring down a villain. The villain has many shapes and faces, but you know him well. He looks like a hobby that consumes your waking hours, a job that keeps you away from home, a dream that keeps you distracted, unfocused, and unhappy, a high-paying career that is killing your family, or a ministry that is booming and keeps you busy 24/7.

You've come to the point where someone's gotta die.

In your case, it's either "him" or your family.

You either plug him or you walk away and continue business as usual. But know this, the villain will eventually catch and destroy your family. That's what villains do.

"Draw."

DAD 2 DAD (ON YOUR OWN OR IN A GROUP)

1. Why do you think dads went from breadwinners to luxury providers and ladder climbers?

2. Do you feel like you have to be a luxury provider?

3. Who puts the most pressure on you to provide "stuff?"

4. What do you think the true cost of a luxury is?

5. What would happen if you didn't provide these luxuries?

6. How high would you have to climb to feel like you had achieved on the ladder of success?

7. How would you feel on your deathbed if you didn't reach that point?

8. Discuss your answers on pages 119-120.

This Looks Like a Job...to Quit!

When we started this book, I asked you to close your eyes, hold your breath and listen. Do it again, only this time put your hand over your heart. Feel that? Each heartbeat brings you closer to the end. Every passing second is irretrievable.

You're faced with a choice: to change directions (if necessary) or to continue on the path you have chosen. I know you need to make some changes (we all do). They may not be huge changes but just a readjustment of priorities. On the other hand, the changes you need to make in your life may be huge.

I know this seems tough, but you can do it! You've got the Power!!!

First thing you need to do is determine how much change is necessary. Let's look at three hypothetical dads...Frank, Don, and Scott.

Frank is a good dad. He's not a workaholic and doesn't go out on the town with the boys, but Frank grew up in a house where his dad took a hands-off approach to parenting, so he does the same.

He comes home from work, reads the paper until dinner time, putters out in the garage or in his garden until bedtime, and reads or watches TV while his wife gets the kids ready for bed.

Frank leads family devotions right after dinner and is a consistent disciplinarian, but he interacts very little with his children and struggles to have fun with his kids. Looking in on his family, you'd think they were the "model" Christian family. The kids are polite and toe the line, although they're a little on the serious side.

After reading this book, Frank realizes he's been withholding affection from his children, needs to have fun with them, and needs to be more approving of their decisions and behavior.

So Frank chooses to change. Here's what he does:

1) He talks with his wife about his decision and asks for her input (already he has scored major points with his wife for admitting what she already knew). She encourages him in his decisions and they talk about some of the things that he can do to implement the changes.

2) Frank makes a conscious effort to touch his children. It feels a little awkward, but he makes sure he touches or hugs each of his children before he heads off to work and once before bedtime. Sometimes his wife has to remind him.

3) Frank decides that instead of reading the paper when he gets home, he will help his wife with the kids so she can get dinner on the table. It will give him some time to be involved in their homework and play with the younger ones.

A month into it though, Frank finds himself slipping back into the habit of reading the paper.

Frank means business about spending time with his kids though, so he cancels his subscription to the newspaper, forcing himself to spend time with his family.

4) Wanting to show more approval, Frank works hard at telling his children that he thinks they're doing a good job. To do that Frank, sticks little Post-It notes on their pillows, lunch sacks, and schoolbooks. In fact, he even stuck one on his teenage son's car telling him he was proud of how he had conducted himself in a tense situation that weekend.

5) Lastly, Frank hooks up with another dad and asks to be held accountable to his decision. This is a tough one. Frank isn't an accountability partner kind of guy. They don't meet weekly or go through any Bible study book, he just asks his friend to ask him about his choices.

Now Frank isn't perfect. He fails more than he succeeds, but he means business and has proven it.

Simple, Not Easy

It's not easy, Dad, but it is simple. All you need to do is admit that there is a problem and then take steps to correct it. Some of the steps will be easy; some will be incredibly difficult. Let me give you another example.

Meet Don. Don is upwardly mobile. He's been a Christian for most of his life, has a good job, and a great family. Don is an achiever. He always has been. He graduated at the top of his class, did well in college, and has worked his way up the corporate ladder earning the respect of his superiors and peers.

The only problem is that Don works a lot. He must in order to keep his job and continue to the next level. Unfortunately, his job takes him away from his family two weeks out of the month. He tries to call home daily, but sometimes has to skip nights because meetings last late or because he's entertaining a client.

When he is in town, he rarely makes it home for dinner and is lucky to be home before most of the kids are in bed. His wife looks like she copes well and doesn't complain of her busy husband's life-style.

"I have broad shoulders," she says. "I knew life would be like this when I married him." The kids have had their moments. They used to beg their dad to stay home but Don notices that they haven't done that for a while and have resolved themselves to the fact that their dad just has to work a lot.

It's this thought that begins to gnaw at Don. The thought has been troubling him for a while, but he doesn't know what to do about it. He is making six figures, with the hope of making a lot more than that if he just sticks with the program.

Then he learns about Father Power and his affect on his children.

He comes to the point where you are now and decides it is time for a change. Here's what he does:

1) Scared spitless, Don prays. He asks for wisdom to do what he has to do and the strength and courage to do it. He

isn't sure where all this will lead but he knows he has to do something.

2) Don asks his wife out on a date and breaks the news to her about what he is thinking. He is pretty sure he will blow her out of the water and is surprised when she starts to cry and tells him that she has been hoping and praying for years for this change of mind. She also says she had given up hope that things would ever change.

For the next three hours and all that weekend, they talk about different options. They talk about his cutting back hours, refusing to travel anymore, and quitting...plus everything in between.

Together, they reach this conclusion: the only way for Don to make a real change is for him to quit his job. They don't have to worry about finances for a while at least. They have a decent savings and have accumulated a healthy stock portfolio.

Still, Don feels like he is ripping his arms from their sockets. His peers think he is crazy, and he wonders the same.

But Don is committed to doing what is best, not what is easiest.

3) That Monday, Don calls his best friend to tell him what he plans to do. There is a stunned silence on the other end of the phone. Mike can't believe that Don would walk away from a high salary and an eventual partnership for his family. As they talk, Mike admires Don for his decision and inwardly wishes he had the guts to do the same.

4) Wanting to strike while the iron is hot; Don gives his 30-day notice before he can change his mind. For the next two days, he is bombarded by questions of disbelief and co-

workers thinking he has flipped. How could he turn his back on success?

5) Over the next 30 days, doubts flood his mind. What has he done? What about his dreams? Will they have to sell their house? Don prays a lot and his wife tells him she thinks he is the bravest man alive.

His kids see that their dad is willing to quit his job so he can spend more time with them. Don doesn't know it, but he has already flexed his Father Power muscles. His decision to put family over work will influence how his children view their jobs and family in the future.

Why?

Father power!!!!

6) Thirty-one days later, Don is unemployed but trusting God for his future employment. He eats breakfast, lunch, and dinner with his family. He is there when his youngest has a nightmare and calls for his daddy. He is there when his teenage daughter asks him about a boy who has shown interest in her. He is there for bike rides, videos nights, and impromptu pillow fights.

He isn't perfect, but he is there. He has chosen the best and future generations will be impacted by his choice. He has doubts, second thoughts, and insecurities, but he has no regrets.

He is a hero to his wife, children, and other dads who watch from the sideline wishing to be just like him.

Why?

Father Power!!!!!!

To Boldly Go Where Few Dads Dare to Go!

I have a flair for the dramatic. I love scenes in movies where normal men do abnormally brave deeds. Usually, the mood is tense and the situation bleak. The odds are 50,000 to 1, but throwing caution and good sense to the wind, the hero appears, takes a deep breath, grabs a sword, and with a scream of defiance throws himself into the fray to defend his family, friend, and the freedom of the world.

Auggggg!!!! He screams...and jumps into the battle.

As he does, all who watch him stand amazed as the hero lives or dies for them. A sense of awe arises and the crowd is never the same after witnessing that act of bravery and courage.

That's what makes him the hero. He's a normal guy doing the abnormal.

Man, I love those moments...probably because I'd like to think I'd be the hero and not a cowering, sniveling guy in the corner.

That's the kind of dad I want to be...a dad who is willing to give up his life for his woman and children. That's Don. That's Frank. But that's not Scott.

One More Example

Let me tell you about Scott. His story is much the same as Don's except that his job doesn't demand any travel. Scott is an over-achiever. He works long hours on the job, and when he isn't at the office, he tackles chores around the house with the same determination and gusto that he gives to his job.

There is always a car to work on, windows to paint, or a lawn to care for. When asked why he works so hard he answers, "We're to work as unto the Lord, aren't we? I just want to do a good job."

Like Don's wife, Scott's wife has prayed for years that he will give more time to their family and know that their children are suffering because of his being gone or busy all the time.

"I don't know what to do." She confesses to a close friend. "I can't nag him anymore. It only makes him angry and defensive."

But then Scott reads this book. He knows he has provoked his children to anger. Inside he has known it for a long time, but now he is face to face with the bold print, and it agrees with him.

So here's what he does:

1) He lets time pass without discussing it with his wife or friend. He prays about it for several days and promises God that he will make changes to be different.

Technically, Chad kept his word to his son.

2) For about a week and a half, Scott leaves work in time to be home for dinner, although he has to make up for it at night on his laptop.

3) He tries to be more involved, but little by little, the feeling fades and he slips back into his old habits.

4) Years pass, and Scott's kids grow up and move away. His sons have careers and families of their own. Learning from their father, that work comes first, they climb corporate ladders, leaving even less time for their family than Scott did.

His daughters marry men much like Scott, but now Scott is able to see how his girls spend most of their time raising a family alone without their husbands' help. To make matters worse, Scott's wife and he have grown distant, and he finds himself alone. He retires and spends much of his time wishing his kids had time to spend with him, but they're to busy pursuing their careers and other "important" things.

CHOOSE FAMILY

So, Dad, who are you most like: Frank, Don, or Scott? You have a choice to make, but it is your choice. I can't make you choose, your wife can't make you choose, and without getting into a theological debate, God won't make you choose.

Father power is yours to use whichever way you choose, but I plead with you to choose family. Take the road often desired but less traveled.

I'm asking you to make the hardest decision you've ever been faced with, but I promise it will be infinitely worth any sacrifice you make now.

It's time for a revival among family men. It's time for the hearts of fathers to turn toward their children. It's time for dads to get down to business and quit their over demanding, family-sacrificing jobs, toss out half finished projects, cancel club memberships, and put long standing dreams on hold. Your family needs you to be the hero. They need you to grab your sword, pull down your helmet, and FIGHT for them!

Father Power!!

THE QUITTERS HANDBOOK

Dad, you must ignore the lies that say, "Only losers quit...Real men stick it out...and Buck up!" As my radio pal Steve Brown often says, "That smells like smoke and is straight from the pit of hell."

Actually, it's the strong, brave men who quit. They quit well paying jobs, walk away from successful ministries, and leave projects unfinished for the sake of their families and that's true nobility.

Be warned, however, that if you quit your job, ministry, or other commitment, people won't understand. In fact, even well meaning Christians will give you a hundred reasons why you shouldn't.

Don't listen to them. Plug your ears and do what God wants you to do and what is right. And "darn" the torpedoes, full steam ahead.

Down deep in your heart, you know it's time for a change. Perhaps you've known it for a long time but have been putting it off. To get the ball rolling, start by doing this:

1) Talk it over with your wife. See if what you're thinking is correct. Does she agree with you or are you just having sympathy pains after reading this book? Maybe you just need to cut something out or cut back. Talk it over and listen to your wife. Together, come up with a good solution.

2) Pray with your wife, pray alone, and tell other Christians who can pray for your decision.

3) Pick a verse from the Bible to serve as your anchor when things get tough.

Here are some good anchors to hold onto:

- *"For I know the plans I have for you," declares the Lord, "plans to prosper you and not harm you, plans to give you hope and a future" (Jeremiah 29:11).*

- *"Have I not commanded you? Be strong and courageous. Do not be terrified; do not be discouraged, for the Lord your God will be with you wherever you go" (Joshua 1:9).*

- *"...I am he who will sustain you. I have made you and I will carry you; I will sustain you and I will rescue you" (Isaiah 46:4b).*

- *"And do not set your heart on what you will eat or drink; do not worry about it. For the pagan world runs after all such things, and your Father knows that you need them. But seek his kingdom, and these things will be given to you as well" (Luke 12:29-31).*

- *"But Jesus immediately said to them: "Take courage! It is I. Don't be afraid"" (Matthew 14:27).*

- *"If any of you lacks wisdom, he should ask God, who gives generously to all without finding fault, and it will be given to him" (James 1:5).*

- *"Trust in the Lord with all your heart and lean not on your own understanding; in all your ways acknowledge him, and he will make your paths straight" (Proverbs 3:5-6).*

4) Tell another guy friend about your decision. Ask him to hold your feet to the fire and pray for you. Give him permission to ask you anything he wants. Ask him to help you make the right decision.

5) If you decide you need to quit your current job, then draw up a resignation notice. There are many samples on the internet.

A) Burn your bridges soon. If this is the right thing to do, make sure you can't undo it. Remember back in history when Cortez discovered the new world? He burned the ships so no one could turn back. Do the same so that when things get scary...and they will, you can't turn back.

B) Write me at: familyman@bnin.net and tell me what you've done. I'd love to share your story to encourage other dads that it can be done. Believe it or not, there is another dad out there who is waiting for you to show him that quitting a job for his family is possible.

C) Start right now by completing the form at the bottom of this page. Then, rip it out of the book and post it somewhere to remind you of the choice you have made.

Let the world know, that I, _____, recognize that I wield a great power over my children. In order to sharpen my children, I realize that I need to_____. There fore, on this date _____, I have determined to Be There!!! May God grant me the wisdom, strength, and courage to do what I need to do for the sake of Father Power!

Well, Dad, thank you for taking your fathering role seriously. You have chosen the best, and though your children may not thank you, allow me to thank you for them. You may be poor, flabby, or drive a rusty car, but you impact your children and the world every day by investing in your family.

Don't worry about doing everything perfectly or consistently. Just be there for your children whenever you can and as much as you can. It won't always be gratifying, fun, or seemingly rewarding.

You will continue to blow it, get angry, and get caught up in things that don't matter, but you will be doing what God commanded through Moses and Paul. You will be training your children for life. They will grow up knowing God loves them and is there for them because **you were there**!!!

WHY?

FATHER POWER.

DAD 2 DAD (ON YOUR OWN OR IN A GROUP)

1. Think about Frank, Don, and Scott...which one do you most identify with?

2. As you ruthlessly examine your life...is there a change that needs to be made?

   How would you rank that change on degree of difficulty from 1-10?

   What will be some of the benefits if you make this change?

   What might be some of the ramifications if you do?

   What are some of the roadblocks that might deter you from making this change?

   Who will be the most supportive?

   Who will be the most critical?

3. What will your children think about the change when they look back in 20 years?

4. What's the first step in making the change?

5. Are you willing to make the change today? If so, write it in the form of a prayer request and then read it to someone.

Appendix

Family Devotions

Just in case you want a tool to help you teach your sons and daughters about God and what He expects from them, here's what I'd suggest.

First, pick a good time and place to meet. For my family, breakfast is the best time. We're all there, and we're not in a hurry to get somewhere. You may choose after dinner or at bedtime to spend some time together in God's word.

Ask your wife what time she thinks would work best for your family.

Scripture

Now that you have a time, you need something to fill that time. Believe me, we've tried everything...Bible stories, Bible lessons, devotionals, and character-building stories, and so far nothing has been "perfect."

That's OK! Your goal is not to make it through a book; your goal is to train and teach your children. So be flexible and diligent. If at first you don't succeed...buy, buy again.

You can always start with the Bible. Read a short "segment" each day and ask the kids what they think it's saying. Don't feel like you have to dissect it or probe its depth, just read it and talk about it for a few minutes.

For some additional resources: go to our website at: www.familymanweb.com (click on the *family devotions* link).

PRAY

We always pray. It's the easy part—usually. Sometimes, we take family prayer requests and pray around the room with each person saying a little prayer. Sometimes, I ask one specific child to lead us in prayer, or I'll pray. Sometimes, the only thing we accomplish is prayer. But that's OK.

As you pray, try to focus on others. Pray for other families, people who need Jesus, and even one another. Often times our prayers sound pretty selfish, "help us to have a good day...help us to be happy and get along...help me to get to go over to Jason's house to play." You get the picture.

ETC.

We also sing at our house...but it comes naturally for me. I used to lead worship at our church, and I have always loved singing. You may not get into that...BUT give it a try. Don't feel as though you have to sing long, old hymns in three-part harmony. Ask the kids what songs they like to sing.

They'll probably pick songs like "Jesus loves me" or some simple choruses. Those are great. I really believe the words are not only pleasing to God but also tune our hearts toward Him and teach truths.

Another thing that we do "sometimes" is Bible memory. This is a great way to train your children for the future and to plant God's truth into their lives where it will remain until it's needed one day.

And just to let you know, I'm memorizing challenged. My kids and wife do much better than I do, but I could care less about memorizing the reference or the exact words. I care about having my children know the truth. They may not know exactly where to find it or the exact wording, but they will have hidden the truth in their hearts.

I print the verse out on my computer, and then we memorize it over the next week or two. The first day I read it, and we talk about what it means. The second day, we memorize the first few words and talk about it a little more. Then each additional day, we memorize a little more until it is finished.

When I think we've got it down, I pick another verse, all the time reviewing the previous verses.

Note: Don't only pick verses that "preach" against the bad habits they have. Balance your selections.

SET THE BAR LOW

Remember, Dad, don't set the bar too high. I used to think we'd all sit around quietly and become more godly together. Instead, our family devotions look like organized chaos. If I haven't disciplined at least one child during our time I feel as though I haven't done my job well.

So don't be disappointed if it doesn't go well, if you skip a few days (or a few weeks), or if the kids don't seem real excited about having devotions. Remember, it's YOUR decision. You're the dad, and you're just doing your job.

Keep at it; start over and over, and don't give up.

About Familyman Ministries

Familyman Ministries' mission is to remind dads about what's most important. They produce books, seminars, audios, and products to help dads be the men, husbands, and fathers they were created to be.

If you would like to learn more about Familyman Ministries or have Todd speak to your group, go to **www.familymanweb.com**.

Other Books for Dads by Todd Wilson

You 'Da Dad - The Best of the Familyman Weekly

For a few years Todd has been sending out a weekly email to thousands of dads of all ages and backgrounds. He encourages them to have pillow fights with their kids, to hunt lightning bugs together, to love unconditionally, and to give without expecting anything in return. This book is a collection of those emails.

The Bathroom Book of Fathering

The Bathroom Book is written in everyday language to remind dads about the importance of family.

You won't find any ten-syllable words or lists of unattainable goals in this book. The chapters are short and filled with simple stories, written by an ordinary dad, who stumbles his way across the minefield called fatherhood. This is a humorous, honest, and real look at kids, parents, and family life.

Sentenced to Care - A Father's Story

A reprobate dad. An innocent son. The perfect crime. A love story you'll never forget.

To avoid paying child support, Billy Luck commits the perfect crime. His son would die, Billy's problems would disappear...and no one would ever know. But the unthinkable happens, and he finds himself *sentenced to care* for the son he had wanted dead and ends up learning how to love someone other than himself.

Order Online at www.familymanweb.com

Every dad needs encouragement in fathering. This weekly e-letter is a lighthearted look into the heart of a dad. It is encouraging, funny, and pathetically real. To sign up, go to **www.familymanweb.com**.